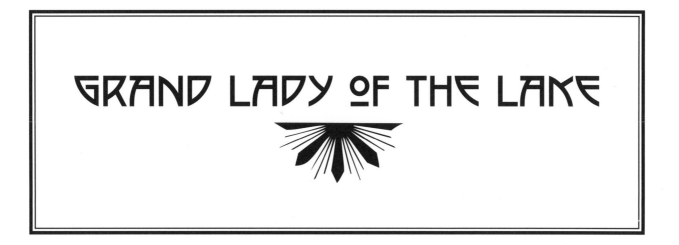

GRAND LADY OF THE LANE

GRAND LADY OF THE LAKE

The Remarkable Legacy of Yellowstone's Lake Hotel

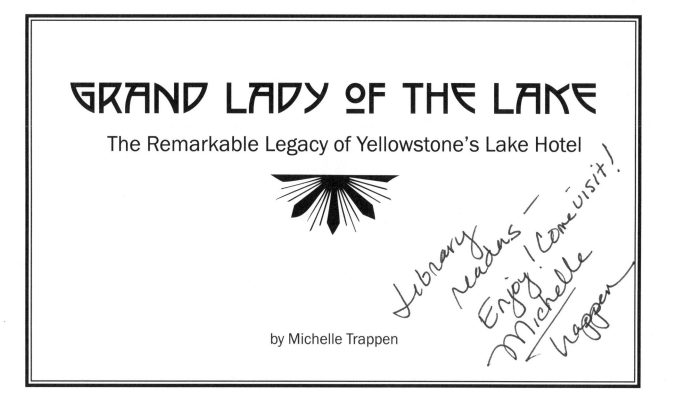

Library
readers —
Enjoy! Come visit!
Michelle
Trappen

by Michelle Trappen

ISBN 13: 978-1-59152-172-3

Published by Red Fox Publications

For more information, write Michelle Trappen, P.O. Box 592, Yellowstone National Park, Wyoming 82190. Or visit www.michelletrappen.com

You may order extra copies of this book by calling Farcountry Press toll free at (800) 821-3874.

Produced by Sweetgrass Books.
PO Box 5630, Helena, MT 59604; (800) 821-3874; www.sweetgrassbooks.com and www.sweetgrassbooks.net.

The views expressed by the author/publisher in this book do not necessarily represent the views of, nor should be attributed to, Sweetgrass Books. Sweetgrass Books is not responsible for the content of the author/publisher's work.

Produced and printed in the United States of America.

20 19 18 17 16   1 2 3 4 5

To Bill,
my father and mentor

To Anna,
my mother and spirit

ACKNOWLEDGMENTS

Thanks to everyone who helped me tackle this project, including: Kat Brekken, for letting me live in her Gardiner, Montana, motorhome in winter 2014, where the book began; Kate Perry, for being my winter 2014 research buddy in the Yellowstone Heritage and Research Center; archivists Shawn Bawden and Hannah Marshall, and museum specialist Brandon Sexton, for helping me track down Lake Hotel material in the research center; Yellowstone park historian Lee Whittlesey, for great advice; my son, Joshua Stein, for shooting the current photographs of the hotel; Mark and Melissa Cox for leasing me their Gardiner, Montana, trailer--with its gorgeous window view of snow-capped Electric Peak—where I wrote the book in winter 2015; Jim and Carol Cutler, for endless support; my sister, Monica Saporito, for designing the book's web site, and for calling me daily to make sure I was still alive; Terry Schmitz, for being my pal and supporting my research in summer 2014; Deanie Carlton, for her continual mentor support; Jen Weaver-Neist, owner of Portland, Oregon's Dame Rocket Press, for editing the bulk of the book; Kathy Springmeyer, director of publications for Sweetgrass Books, for saving the day and all of her sage advice; designer Chris Purcell, for making the book's interior beautiful; author and editor Greg Mandel, for stepping in, last-minute, to help with editing chores. A special thanks to Leslie and Ruth Quinn, for taking time out of their busy summer schedules to review the book for historical accuracy. Most of all, a tip-of-the-top-hat to the late Harry Child and Robert Reamer, for making the Lake Hotel a national treasure.

CONTENTS

INTRODUCTION

When I first moved to Yellowstone in August, 2012, it was never with the intention of writing a book about the Lake Hotel. In fact, I was pretty annoyed when I discovered I would be working at the Lake Yellowstone Hotel (its newer name—I will explain later). I desperately wanted to land at the Old Faithful Inn, where I had stayed on a one-night whirlwind park tour in 2000. As I tell guests, Old Faithful Inn is "jaw dropping." Everybody knows about Old Faithful.

But the Lake Hotel?

My mood soured more when I arrived at the hotel. I had been hired as "kitchen help," which I assumed meant I would be chopping vegetables, making salads—things like that. Ah, but no. I was assigned to the dish pit, to scrub grubby plates and bowls, before feeding everything into a giant conveyer belt dishwasher. I have toiled as a journalist since age 14; my last job, I worked twenty one years as a feature writer for *The Oregonian* in Portland, Oregon. I was a sitter, not a stander. Yet here I stood for eight hours, in my Chef Boyardee outfit, washing dishes.

My adult children made bets on how fast I would quit. Not only was I scrubbing dishes (my Number One dreaded house chore), I was living in a dorm—with a twenty-one-year-old roommate named Toast (an international employee from Taiwan, this was the American name she had chosen). Dorm life in my 50s definitely sounded like a recipe for disaster, especially coupled with dishpan hands.

But what my children, my parents, my friends back home in Portland did not realize is that Yellowstone casts a spell on those who come for more than a few vacation days. It becomes what my friend and fellow Yellowstoner, Terry Schmitz, calls "magic."

Two weeks after I arrived, a supervisor performed magic and got me out the dish pit. I was transferred to the employee dining room (better known as the EDR), where I served food and mopped floors. It was hardly glamorous, but it definitely beat the dish pit.

Somewhere in that time frame, I went on the Lake Hotel's free historic tour. I loved the tour, and later sought out tour guide, Linda Adams, in the employee dining room. Adams, it turned out, not only gave hotel tours, she also drove the Lake Butte Sunset tour in the historic yellow bus. And she worked part-time on the hotel's activities desk, helping guests plan their days in the park.

I wanted that job!

Fate, of course, dances in our lives. I came to Yellowstone to heal, to recover from the loss of my career (newspapers are dying) and the death of a man I loved dearly. And so I listened, a bit breathlessly, as Linda told me how she would not be returning to Yellowstone the following summer, and how her job would be available. That's when she asked me, the lowly kitchen swab, if I might be interested.

"Ay!" I must have bellowed.

Linda called her boss that same day, from a pay phone in the lobby of Goldeneye, the older person dorm at the Lake. I shamelessly eavesdropped. Linda knew nothing about me beyond our chat at dinner, yet she made me sound like a champion. I felt stunned, and gleeful. Writing this, I realize how much I owe Linda, who I have not seen or been in contact with since that summer. Neither one of us had a clue that a book would emerge from that pivotal moment.

The following spring, in May, 2013, I found myself training for my concierge/tour guide/bus driving job at the Lake Yellowstone Hotel. The hotel was renamed in the 1980s after a major, life-saving renovation. Now, though, out of respect for the hotel's 125th anniversary in 2016, I have decided to mostly use the original name, Lake Hotel, throughout this book.

That summer, I conducted hotel tours five nights a week—but really, I knew little about the long yellow building. Fortunately, I had a thirty-two page history book, *Plain to Fancy: The Story of the Lake Hotel*, by Barbara Dittl and Joanne Mallmann to use as a guide. Unfortunately, guests could not purchase the book, first published in 1987, because it was out of print and unavailable.

That's when I first thought about writing about the hotel. Once a writer, always a writer, I suppose. The fact that the hotel approached its 125th anniversary also fueled my thinking.

It has been a long journey, researching and writing about the longest standing hotel originally built in a national park. In the beginning, I intended to crank out something simple, but the more I learned, the more I wanted to share. Not that I know everything: information about the Lake Hotel—especially early history—is either scattered far and wide, or non-existent.

So I admit I don't know everything. This book is a work in progress. As I learn more, as others share what they know, subsequent editions will include that information.

Let me please say: Enjoy. And if you have a question, want to tell me what you think, or make a correction, I'm easy to find: I'm Michelle, the red-headed concierge/hotel tour guide/historic yellow bus driver.

The author of *Grand Lady of the Lake*.

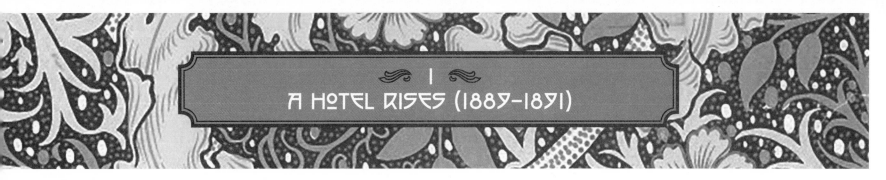

ruth be known, Yellowstone became America's first national park because a railroad saw the keen potential for tourism, and helped convince Congress to preserve and protect more than two million acres of land.

And the Lake Hotel finally got built between 1889 and 1891 because a railroad, tired of endless delays from park leaders, put up the needed money.

And the bulk of the Lake Hotel's earliest high-brow guests arrived because a railroad provided the transportation to reach Yellowstone.

So the story of the Lake Hotel really starts with the Northern Pacific Railroad and its quest to turn Yellowstone into a worthy destination for mostly East Coast and European upper-crust travelers. Railroad-generated brochures waxed on about "Wonderland," the magical park in America's rugged west where geysers exploded, waterfalls plunged, and wild animals roamed.

The brochures did not lie: Yellowstone abounded with natural wonders. What it woefully lacked were decent roads and hotels—two key features needed to woo guests accustomed to plush lodging like Le Meurice in Paris or The Savoy in London.

By the late 1880s, the park roads had progressed enough for hotels to be built, but the Yellowstone Park Association dragged its heels on construction. Finally, work began on three hotels in 1889, but complications ensued, requiring the Northern Pacific to kick in at least $60,000—nearly $1.6 million in today's money.[2] The money paid off with the opening of the Canyon Hotel in 1890, and the Fountain Hotel and the Lake Hotel in 1891.

Sadly, the Canyon and Fountain Hotels were long ago demolished. And the Northern Pacific Railroad, along with other railroad companies that eventually delivered passengers to Yellowstone's borders, vanished after World War II. By all accounts, the Lake Hotel also should be gone, a relic of park history; several times in its 125 years of existence, park leaders planned its demolition. Fate and luck kept the hotel alive.

So here's the story of the Lake Hotel, now known as the Lake Yellowstone Hotel. It's a bumpy ride, much like the travel stagecoach passengers endured in the early days. But it's also the story of a survivor: no hotel has stood in a national park longer than the Lake Hotel.

The Grand Lady of the Lake.

Opposite: The original Lake Hotel looks rather simple compared to the current hotel. But its fifty-one guest bedrooms trumped the rugged tent camp that served the area between 1887 and 1891. As Park Superintendent Moses Harris noted in his 1887 annual report: "A domicile in tents at an altitude of 7,000 or 8,000 feet, where heavy frosts prevail every night, can, by no stretch of the imagination, be made to appear comfortable. It may, as a novelty, be endured for one or two nights, but at the end of that period, the average summer visitor prefers to seek a lower altitude and the comforts of a good hotel."[1] [Photo courtesy of the Montana Historical Society Research Center]

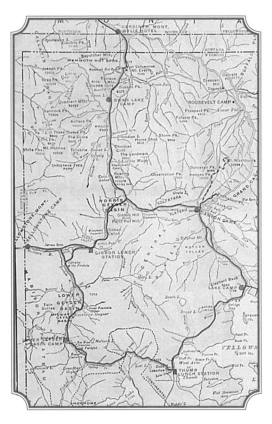

When Philetus Norris became Yellowstone's second superintendent in 1877, just thirty-two miles of road existed in the park. When he left in 1882, the road system had been expanded to more than one hundred and fifty crude miles. But it wasn't until 1891 that stagecoaches could actually circle the park's lower loop. This map shows how stagecoaches could leave Mammoth Hot Springs (at the top of the map) and roll down the park's left side, circle around the bottom past the Lake Hotel and up to Canyon before looping around to the Norris Geyser Basin—and back up to Mammoth. (This map was created by the Wylie Camping Company, which offered lower cost accommodations at tent camps throughout the park. Lake Lodge, located next door to the Lake Hotel, started as a Wylie camp). *[Photo courtesy of the National Park Service]*

The Long Road to the Lake Hotel

Lodging might have improved sooner—Yellowstone leaders certainly recognized the need—but transporting building materials and labor into a tree-clogged park bigger in size than Delaware and Rhode Island combined proved a near impossible task.

Indeed, Nathaniel Langford, the park's first superintendent, refused to issue leases to a number of entrepreneurs who wished to erect hotels because no roads existed to transport guests, and Congress wasn't coughing up the cash to build them.

During the park's first years of existence, guests could explore only on foot or horseback, or in wagons that bounced over rough trails, which also required frequent walking or wading of rivers and streams. Consider the 1880 trip of Robert and Carrie Adell Strahorn, who traveled four hundred miles by horseback through Yellowstone. In her book, *Fifteen Thousand Miles by Stage*, Carrie writes:

"There are no adjectives in our language that can properly define the public highway that was cut through heavy timber over rolling ground, with stumps left from two to twenty inches above ground; and instead of grading around a hill, it went straight to the top on one side and straight down the other...We had to abandon the light wagon and returned for a new start on horseback, for it was impossible to get any conveyance over the stumpy road."[3]

It wasn't until 1878 that Philetus Norris, Yellowstone's second superintendent, laid the groundwork for the park's 142-mile Grand Loop Road. But construction inched along, slowed by a lack of funding and the project's sheer size.

Fortuitously, when the Lake Hotel opened in 1891, the section of the Grand Loop Road that linked the Old Faithful area with Yellowstone Lake was finally completed. Now guests could truly circle the park in a stagecoach, traveling from hotel to hotel, much like a cruise ship sails from port to port.

Two decades after the park's creation, Yellowstone finally had a decent road system—and hotels to match.

1889: Remote Location, Supply Woes, Construction Blunders

In 1889, work finally began on the Lake Hotel.

What a spectacular year that must have been, in terms of park activity. Three much-needed hotels were simultaneously under construction: the Canyon Hotel, located at the Grand Canyon of the Yellowstone; the Fountain Hotel, which rose east of the Fountain Paint Pot in the Lower Geyser Basin; and the Lake Hotel, which sprawled across a bluff overlooking magnificent Yellowstone Lake.

Park roads had improved by 1889, but by today's standards, they were barely more than rutted paths. A good rainstorm turned dirt to mush. The sheer task of transporting endless building materials, heavy furniture, as well as

food and shelter for the construction workers relied heavily on favorable weather.

Also, almost everything needed to build and furnish the three hotels had to be transported on Northern Pacific Railroad from St. Paul, Minnesota, or Portland, Oregon. Materials were loaded onto supply wagons at the train depot in Cinnabar, Montana (a town that no longer exists), eight miles north of Mammoth Hot Springs. Imagine the number of heavily laden wagons that must have rolled from Cinnabar up the curvy hill to Mammoth Hot Springs, and then on to the distant Fountain, Canyon, and Lake building sites.

Supply wagons crisscrossed the park between 1889 and 1891, transporting everything from hammers and nails to kitchen appliances to the construction sites at the Canyon, Fountain, and Lake Hotels. *[Photo courtesy of the National Park Service]*

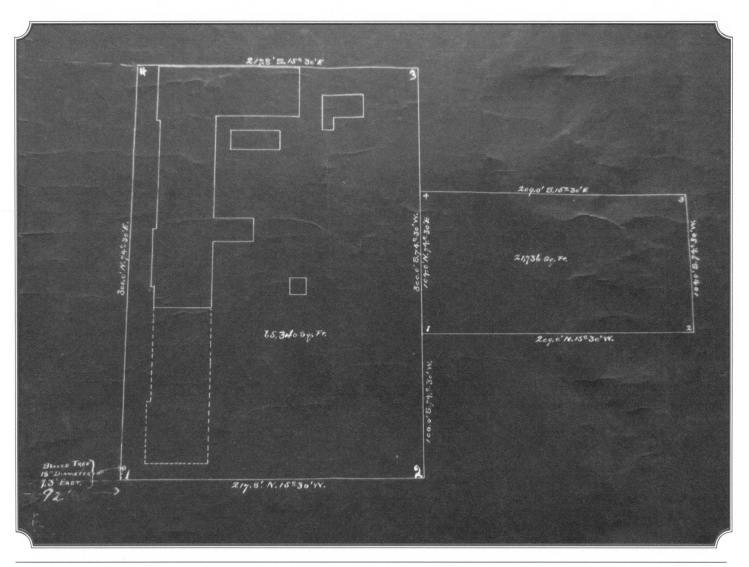

This blueprint shows the original dimensions of the Lake Hotel, designed by architect Nicholas T. Haller, who had done previous work for the Northern Pacific Railroad. The hotel faced Yellowstone Lake (located on the left); a short, three-floor bathroom wing extended to the rear (center right); and an ell wing held the dining room, attached kitchen, and baking areas. Bedrooms lined the hotel's second- and third-floor corridors. The two small buildings next to the ell wing were the engine room (right), and icehouse (bottom). The small square in the center was a water tank, and the large attached rectangle of land located at right contained the hotel's barn. The dashed lines on the bottom illustrate the hotel's current mid-section, which park leaders postponed building until 1903–04. *[Photo courtesy of the Montana Historical Society Research Center]*

> **"** I am told...that....there are many places in the foundation that [one] can today push over with his foot. **"**

Work actually started on the hotel before the official blueprint had been approved by John Noble, Secretary of the Department of the Interior. In fact, when the blueprint finally showed up in May of 1890, it caused quite a stir, because the hotel's architect, Nicholas T. Haller of Washington, D.C., had never been to the building site. Park Superintendent F. A. Boutelle wrote Noble, explaining how the specifications had "been prepared by some architect employed at Washington without any knowledge or consideration of the material now on the ground...The specifications will have to be modified or the work delayed."[4]

By this point, much work had already been completed on the hotel under the direction of R. R. Cummins, the Yellowstone Park Association (YPA) construction superintendent. Workers quarried rock from within the park to lay the hotel's foundation, and a temporary, onsite sawmill cut the board lumber used in the building's frame. Work appeared to be on schedule, so park leaders predicted the Lake Hotel would open in the summer of 1890.

But problem after problem haunted the project. Master builder Cummins could not always be on site; he was also managing the Canyon and Fountain hotel projects. In his absence, Ela C. Waters, the YPA's general manager of hotels, ran the show—and sometimes ineptly. It was Waters, for instance, who supervised the installation of the hotel's rubble-stone foundation. For whatever reason, Waters allowed workers to lay the foundation over a bumpy surface of tree stumps and clay—a debacle that YPA Comptroller E. C. Buchanan learned about in November 1889. "I am told...that...there are many places in the foundation that [one] can today push over with his foot," he reported to Northern Pacific Railroad officials.[5]

The project was further hampered by the tardy arrival of building supplies. Builders had to wait on a long list of materials, including major items, like most of the oak Queen Anne staircase; two hundred feet of four-inch steam pipe, and the wire in Edison's electric lighting system that would illuminate the building.[6]

The delays gave workmen extra time on their hands, which led to trouble. Apparently the plasterers drank too much that summer, triggering a telegram to YPA General Manager W. G. Pearce, imploring him to "Please send, as soon as possible, good plasterers...wages $3.50 per day and board... to take place of dissatisfied whiskey fiends."[7]

The construction issues and supply delays ultimately convinced YPA leaders to modify the blueprints, and postpone construction of a 120-foot wing (that today is the hotel's mid-section). They obviously believed it would be added sooner than later, because that side of the hotel was left unfinished (with rough logs). But the wing would not be realized for twelve more years.

Finally, the hotel was near completion and ready for furnishings. As the YPA's general manager of hotels, E. C. Waters was entrusted with the task of picking the couches and chairs, lamps, and other furnishings. Alas, he chose poorly. YPA Assistant General Manager W. G. Johnson declared the furniture "not good enough for the Lake Hotel—or any other hotel in the park, for that matter."[8]

New furniture was ordered and park leaders fired Waters (for problems with the Lake Hotel

and other infractions). Waters, though, proved resilient, and almost immediately bounced back as the first manager of the Yellowstone Lake Boat Company, located next door to the Lake Hotel.

Excitement must have mounted as workers nailed pine clapboard on the hotel's exterior, and—according to published accounts—painted it a soft yellow. Historical records don't verify that color, and painters who toiled on the hotel's 2012–14 renovation think it may have been painted white originally. It's hard to say, because black-and-white photographs don't reveal the truth. However, by the late 1890s, the hotel definitely wore yellow paint, and it's been yellow ever since (though some park leaders in the 1970s advocated repainting the hotel gray or brown to better blend in with the woodsy environment).

Topping the original hotel, much like a tiara, was an observation deck, also known as a widow's walk. No photos show guests or anybody else standing on it. Most likely the structure was built so hotel employees could scramble up there in case of a chimney fire, and dump sand down to quell flames.

Finally, in July 1891, after two years of sweat and struggles, the Lake Hotel opened its doors to guests.

The hotel was originally built on a rubble-stone foundation, some of which is still visible today. This particular section of stone is found near the dining room's east end. Over the years, the hotel has undergone multiple renovations, and the foundation has been repaired and strengthened with modern materials. *[Photo courtesy of the author]*

A Room with a View

With its gorgeous view of the Absaroka Mountain Range and close proximity to great fishing, it's easy to understand why early park leaders chose the bluff above Yellowstone Lake as the choice spot to build the Lake Hotel.

The lake mesmerizes, stretching the eye to absorb the largest body of fresh water found at 7,700 feet in North America. It's a kaleidoscopic view, calm and misty in the morning but often whipped and white-capped by afternoon. In May and early June, the thick ice that encapsulates the lake all winter cracks and shifts until the wind sweeps it down the Yellowstone River.

The original Lake Hotel certainly did not compare to the upscale East Coast resorts that many of Yellowstone's discerning travelers frequented. But the three-story hotel offered fifty-one modestly furnished rooms and a host of modern-day amenities, like electric lights and steam heat—luxuries after a rugged day of travel in the park.

Guests would have entered through double doors on the hotel's lake-facing front side and checked in at the registration desk, then located where the lobby fireplace now burns. Brass key in hand, guests climbed the Queen Anne–style staircase to rooms on the second and third floors. Unlike today's main staircase, which has a south–north entry, guests started their ascent from a west–east direction. Porters handled the bags or trunks, which were transported upstairs by a small elevator located at the porter desk (then located in the area now occupied by the back door entry hall).

Guest rooms sprawled across the hotel's main section (now known as west wing, or the Old House) and through the ell wing, located on the floors above the kitchen area. Each room came equipped with a white porcelain washbasin and a large, matching porcelain pitcher, which guests (or a maid) could fill with water from the communal restrooms located down the hall. A mirror hung above each room's

marble-topped washstand, adorned by towel bars on either side.

The luckiest guests occupied one of the choice lake-facing rooms, but back-facing rooms offered sumptuous forest views and the occasional bear sighting.

A higher income level did not secure anyone a private bathroom; no one had such a luxury. At that point in history, private toilets were extremely rare, though increasing in popularity. Rooms came equipped with chamber pots, and on all three floors, guests shared communal washrooms, water closets, and bathing rooms.

In 1901, management reconfigured hotel space to somehow squeeze in another seventeen rooms, but by and large, the hotel remained the same—small and simple—until architect Robert Reamer debuted his iconic Colonial Revival look in 1904.

1895: Layout of the Original Lake Hotel

The Lake Hotel has changed its appearance many times in its long lifetime. These hand-drawn schematics show what the hotel looked like in 1895.

In those days, the sunroom and gift shop did not exist, and the dining room was half its current size. The hotel's east side ended where today's ground-floor hallway begins, near the registration desk.

The following descriptions, with corresponding numbers, explain the original hotel.

- **Dining room (1, first-floor diagram)**—The original dining room was located where today's dining room sits. It was attached to the north-jutting ell wing, which housed a ground-floor kitchen, bakery, pantry, storage room, and help's hall.

- **Ordinary room (2)**—This large lake-facing room may have been the equivalent of a Victorian morning room, or a ladies' receiving room, that guests used for daytime activities and recreations like writing and socializing. It was later converted into two-bedroom suites.

- **Unmarked room (3)**—This room is designated as an "ordinary room" on other documents. It likely was used for socializing, and perhaps was used as a waiting area for the dining room.

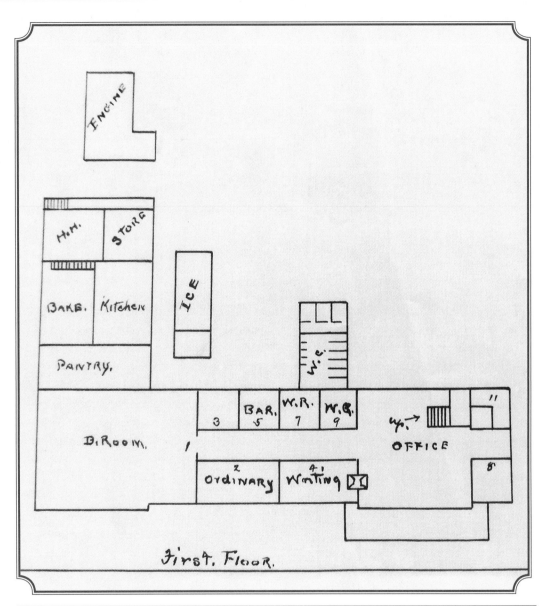

[Diagrams courtesy of the Montana Historical Society Research Center]

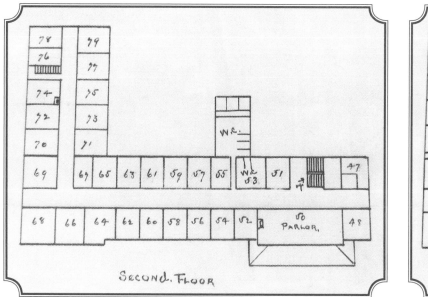

Second Floor

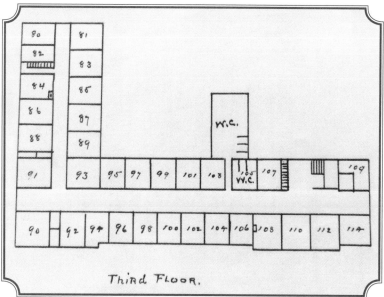

Third Floor.

- **Writing room (4)**—This room featured a two-sided fireplace, meaning flames crackled in the writing room and on the opposite side, facing the lobby (what's labeled the "office"). In 1895, this large space was split in two to hold both a bedroom suite and a writing room.

- **Barroom (5)**—The bar first appeared in 1895. Up to that point, government rules prohibited saloons or barrooms in park hotels. George Anderson, then the park's acting military superintendent, lobbied for a rule change that allowed park bars, and finally succeeded.

- **Wine room (7)**—What sounds like a lovely place to sample wines was actually the bartending room, where drinks got mixed and placed on trays for

serving. The beverages could only be taken from the wine room to the bar through an adjoining door. Alcohol was not served or allowed anywhere else in the hotel.

- **Bedroom (8)**—Located on the east side of the lobby, near the porter's desk, it's possible that the hotel manager had this bedroom. The original hotel ended at this east wall when park leaders decided to hurry things up, and not extend the planned wing.

- **Water closet (9)**—The outer room served as a communal washroom, and the inner room a "water closet," which held toilets. Another space in the inner room offered bathing tubs. Each of the hotel's three floors had the same setup. Bedrooms came equipped with chamber pots.

- **Porter (11)**—This room was located in the entry hall, by today's main back entrance. The hotel's first-ever elevator, situated here, was used to take luggage upstairs.

- **Lobby ("office" area)**—Guests disembarked stagecoaches and entered the hotel from the front, on the lake-facing side. They checked in at the registration desk, which was found in front of today's fireplace.

- **Parlor (50, second-floor diagram)**—Found upstairs, above the lobby. Guests could sit here and enjoy a fireplace-lit setting. Double doors led outside for a veranda view of the lake.

The Picture Tells the Story

This photograph reveals so much about the early Lake Hotel, which was valued at $46,000 in 1895—about $1.3 million in today's dollars.[9] Among the observations:

1. The rough-hewn wall. Unlike the rest of the hotel, which was finished with pine clapboard, the east end was essentially patched over in anticipation of later completion. But twelve years would pass before architect Robert Reamer finally expanded the hotel.

2. The wooden front porch, where guests climbed in or out of the stagecoaches, served as an entry, but also as a place to sit and visit—or stand and jaw, like the two men shown on the porch's right end.

3. The upstairs veranda offered guests a better vantage of Yellowstone Lake and the distant Absaroka Mountain Range.

4. Four-by-four, double-sash windows dominated the early hotel. The rope-and-pulley windows are still in use today, but the hotel now features a wide assortment of window types, with some containing as many as eighteen panes.

When park leaders decided to not complete the east end of the hotel, they had workmen finish off that side with rough log siding—anticipating the wing would extend eventually. *[Photo courtesy of the National Park Service, Yellowstone National Park YELL#129467]*

In 1891, engineers finally completed the lower loop of the park's road system, enabling guests to more efficiently circle Yellowstone on what was known as the "Grand Tour." The Lake, Fountain, and Canyon hotels had also been completed, offering travelers far better accommodations than ever before.

And so began what some may consider the Lake Hotel's golden age—a slower, gentler era when Yellowstone Observation Wagons rolled guests from hotel to hotel, unveiling a diorama of natural wonders along the way.

The one-night stay at the Lake Hotel offered the quiet spot on the tour—the place where guests could fully unwind and just absorb nature. Here, travelers strolled in the woods, took a boat ride on the lake, or just sat and rocked in chairs on the broad front porch.

It would have been a night to remember.

All Aboard!

The Lake Hotel may have opened up for business in 1891, but getting there took some doing.

Unless the guest lived close enough to Yellowstone to ride in by wagon or horseback, the trip required train travel on the Northern Pacific Railroad (years later, competing railroads offered options to other park entrances). Earliest guests began their journeys from the East Coast,

St. Paul, Minnesota in the Midwest, or Portland, Oregon, in the West, but all ended up in Livingston, Montana (sixty miles north of Gardiner, Montana—Yellowstone's north entrance).

In 1891, most of Yellowstone's guests hailed from the East Coast or Europe, and they had money. The all-inclusive trip from St. Paul or Portland cost $110 per person, around $2,850 in today's dollars. It was a luxury most Americans could not afford: According to the National Bureau of Economic Research, the average wage in 1890 for a sixty-hour work week ranged from $9.06 for a common laborer to $19.32 for a carpenter.[2]

Those who could afford the trip, though, traveled in style. The Northern Pacific pampered its first-class passengers, providing plush velvet or leather seats, steam heat, fresh linen daily, and porters who catered to every whim. The ticket price covered round-trip transportation, one double berth in a Pullman sleeping car, and dining-car meals—as well as transportation, lodging, and meals for five and one quarter days in Yellowstone.

When guests arrived in Livingston, they transferred to Northern Pacific's Park Branch Line for the final two-hour chug to a rather desolate depot in Cinnabar, Montana. Ideally, the train would have continued on the final three miles to Gardiner, but a land lease dispute with a gentleman named Robert E. "Jim Buckskin" Cutler prevented construction of a far more convenient depot there until 1902.

Opposite: After guests arrived in Livingston, Montana, they transferred to Northern Pacific Railroad's Park Branch Line (shown here in 1896) and traveled fifty-five miles to the original depot in Cinnabar, Montana. According to former park historian Aubrey Haines, earliest journeys sometimes included impromptu stops—like when "the engineer, with revolver in hand, pursued two prairie chickens he had sighted."[1] [Photo courtesy of the Montana Historical Society Research Center]

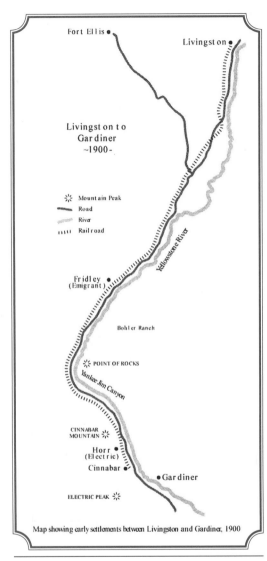

Livingston to
Gardiner
~1900~

Fort Ellis •
Livingston •

Mountain Peak
Road
River
Railroad

Yellowstone River

Fridley •
(Emigrant)

Bohler Ranch

POINT OF ROCKS
Yankee Jim Canyon

CINNABAR
MOUNTAIN

Horr •
(Electric)
Cinnabar •   • Gardiner

ELECTRIC PEAK

Map showing early settlements between Livingston and Gardiner, 1900

This map illustrates the Park Branch Line between Livingston and Gardiner, Montana. The train long ago stopped shuttling guests to Yellowstone, but the track bed still parallels US Route 89 through Paradise Valley to the park's north entrance. *[Photo courtesy of the Montana Historical Society Research Center]*

Stagecoaches Gallop Guests Up Into the Park

When the train finally reached the now non-existent Cinnabar depot (then located southwest of today's Corwin Springs), guests disembarked to find a tiny, dusty town—awash with everything Old West: saloons, a general store, a blacksmith shop, a livery stable and a shack of a hotel, all out in the middle of nowhere. Here, while fending off souvenir hawkers selling everything from Indian artifacts to Yellowstone-related trinkets, the guests boarded powerful Tally-Ho stagecoaches, the first of two types of coaches they would travel in as they toured Yellowstone.

Manufactured by Abbot-Downing of Concord, New Hampshire, each Tally-Ho required six

Guests pull up to the National Hotel riding in (or piled on!) a Tally-Ho stagecoach. This turn-of-the-century photo shows at least fifteen passengers, but a Tally-Ho could actually seat up to thirty-five passengers—an astonishing number for the size of the vehicle. And yes, those are seats mounted on top of the coach (a popular spot). *[Photo courtesy of the National Park Service]*

horses to pull passengers up the windy, steep hill between Gardiner and Mammoth Hot Springs—the jumping-off spot for the Grand Tour. Back then, today's river-hugging road that connects Gardiner and Mammoth did not exist; instead, the road started where today's north entrance ranger station is located. The Tally-Hos bounced along, through the sagebrush-dotted hills, until making a final descent behind the National Hotel (current location of the Mammoth Hot Springs Hotel).

The National Hotel. *[Photo courtesy of the National Park Service, Yellowstone National Park YELL#11477]*

Want to ride in a replica Tally-Ho stagecoach?

Xanterra Parks and Resorts (the company that manages Yellowstone) offers stagecoach rides several times daily, June through August. The forty-five minute, round-trip tour departs from the Roosevelt Corral, in the park's eastern section, and travels to nearby Pleasant Valley. It's a perfect outing for young 'uns and anybody with a curiosity about Yellowstone's stagecoach past.[3]

First Night: The National Hotel

Guests received their first real taste of Yellowstone and the Grand Tour at the National Hotel in Mammoth Hot Springs. Built in 1883 (but not finished until 1886), the sprawling building boasted four stories and featured a gentlemen's room, a ladies' parlor, and a spacious dining room. But most impressive—at least, according to a writer with the weekly *Bozeman Avant Courier*—was the on-site museum: "It will attract the curious multitudes...and the oddities, petrifactions, and thousand-and-one curiosities displayed here will prove quite a card for the farsighted managers."[4]

After guests checked in, they likely headed outside to explore the nearby travertine terraces and steamy thermal pools. Then, guests could actually climb on the chalky-white terraces and pose for photographs (strictly prohibited today!).

Young, sun-leathered cowboys or ranchers—likely from Montana or Wyoming—grasped the reins but also served as tour guides, explaining nature as it rolled into view. The drivers had cool western nicknames like "Society Red" (loved dancing; maybe a redhead), "Crying Jack" (weepy looking), and "Scattering Jesus" (nervous, flighty, perhaps religious).[5] *[Photo courtesy of the Montana Historical Society Research Center]*

Passengers often wore linen duster coats (yellow for males, gray for females) to protect their clothing, hats or shaker bonnets to guard their hair, and bandannas or scarves to shield their mouths and noses.

Guests also delighted in filling small souvenir bottles with thermal water or buying "coated specimens" from Ole Anderson. The concessionaire had an unusual business that no longer exists: transforming ordinary objects into travertine-coated souvenirs. Anderson took horseshoes, pinecones—even objects provided by guests—and placed them on a rack that he then positioned beneath the cascading terrace waters. The mineral-rich waters coated the objects and turned them alabaster white.

After absorbing the glories of Mammoth Hot Springs, Grand Tour guests woke the next morning and gathered on the hotel's veranda to board the four-horse Yellowstone Observation Wagons. These bright-yellow coaches were specially designed for touring, each featuring a covered top; open sides, and four forward-facing benches (the driver, and two passengers, occupied one bench). Up to eleven passengers were assigned

to each wagon, and they remained with that driver throughout the tour.

Excitement must have mounted as the coaches took off, headed for the Fountain Hotel in the Lower Geyser Basin. Coaches departed at intervals, to minimize dust, which could quickly cloud up the view during the summer. Passengers often wore linen duster coats (yellow for males, gray for females) to protect their clothing, hats or shaker bonnets to guard their hair, and bandannas or scarves to shield their mouths and noses.

Travel by coach had its share of challenges, especially on rutted or muddy roads; some stretches required guests to get out and walk— or worse, push. But the lovely scenery and frequent stops to observe animals and other natural features no doubt softened the hardships.

It was all a part of the "Wild West" experience.

Ole Anderson used the natural powers of the travertine terraces at Mammoth Hot Springs to transform ordinary objects into souvenirs. Guests chose an item in Anderson's store (or provided one of their own) at the beginning of the Grand Tour and picked up the finished souvenir at tour's end. This horseshoe is an example of Anderson's work. [Photo courtesy of the National Park Service, Yellowstone National Park YELL#119048-02]

The Great Stagecoach Robbery

Stagecoach robberies in America's sprawling west were common in the early 1900s, and Yellowstone had its share. Guns were strictly prohibited in the park, which made Grand Tour coaches easy pickings for a robber, who simply jumped out from behind trees, cocked a gun, and demanded valuables.

Perhaps the greatest stagecoach robbery in Yellowstone history happened in August of 1908. On a single day, a lone highwayman stopped twelve stagecoaches en route from the Upper Geyser Basin to the Lake Hotel, robbing 125 passengers of all ages. The robber wore bluish-brown overalls, a brown shirt, and a soft felt hat; and he carried an automatic rifle. He also had a German accent.[6]

Victims held a meeting that evening at the Lake Hotel to draft a grievance, stating they had been "insulted, struck, robbed of money and valuables to the extent of about twenty-hundred dollars."[7] They also drafted a series of resolutions that maintained their park passage should be peaceable; and that if a neglect of duty had occurred, they should be compensated for their losses.[8]

**Listen here, baby dear,
I'm afraid to go out in the Park.
Every day there's a robbery, they say;
They don't wait till "after dark."**

**Stopped the coach at half-past nine,
Robbed everyone in line.
There's no place like home, dear;
I'm afraid to go out in the Park.[10]**

*—Composed by Miss Halle
Memphis, Tennessee, 1908*

NEWS BULLETIN, Aug. 28, 1908— T. A. Edison, scientist and inventor, who passed through here tonight [by train] on his way to Yellowstone Park, says, "Recent holdup of over one hundred tourists in Wonderland will doubtless keep hundreds of tourists from visiting [the] Park this year." Mr. Edison said there are a number of people who changed their plans and decided not to visit the Park after hearing about the holdup.[9]

[Photo courtesy of Shutterstock]

Next Stop: The Fountain Hotel

On their first full day in the park (day two of the tour), guests rolled south from the National Hotel toward the geyser basins, passing through the majestic Golden Gate Canyon, observing the gleaming Obsidian Cliff (and learning how the Sheepeater tribe made arrowheads), and listening to the bellowing fumaroles of Roaring Mountain. Their destination: the Fountain Hotel, located near today's Fountain Paint Pot in the Lower Geyser Basin.

The F-shaped Fountain Hotel was known as the sister to the Lake Hotel because they shared design characteristics. But the Fountain was much larger, holding one hundred and thirty-three rooms, enough to accommodate two hundred and fifty guests. The Fountain also

hosted grand balls, attracting not just guests but the park's military personnel. Such affairs were held in the dining room, which doubled as a ballroom, and nightly dancing took place in the drawing room.

Beyond dancing, guests could also gather around a crackling ground-floor fireplace or (after 1895) sip libations in a cozy bar. But the hotel's most appreciated amenity had to be the natural hot-spring water piped in from nearby Leather Pool, affording guests the luxury of hot mineral baths.

Before Old Faithful Inn opened in 1904, Grand Tour guests stayed at the Fountain two nights, allowing plenty of time to explore the geyser basins and, of course, to watch Old Faithful spout. But no one needed to leave

The Fountain Hotel. *[Photo courtesy of the National Park Service, Yellowstone National Park YELL#160]*

the hotel to view a gusher. The hotel's expansive porch and second-floor veranda offered dead-on views of nearby Fountain Geyser, which could blast sixty feet skyward!

These stunning veranda views are now a thing of the past. The hotel opened in 1891, the same year as the Lake Hotel, but it closed after the summer season of 1916, the first full year that the automobile was allowed in Yellowstone. Park leaders decided the short distance between the Fountain Hotel and Old Faithful Inn negated the need for two geyser-basin hotels. Sadly, the Fountain was demolished in 1927.

Next Stop:
West Thumb and the *Zillah*

On the fourth day of the Grand Tour, the coaches lumbered away from the Fountain Hotel and headed south to steamy West Thumb on Yellowstone Lake. Here, guests enjoyed lunch— and pondered their next mode of transportation.

The Grand Tour included stage transportation, but at this crossroads, guests had the option of traveling the next leg of the journey on a steamer named the *Zillah*. The boat ride took them from West Thumb to the Lake Hotel, on the lake's north shore. It cost each traveler an additional $2.50, which some considered pricey (around $65 in today's dollars). [11] But after three days of clattery, dusty travel, the steamer must have sounded heavenly—especially when coach drivers actively pitched the excursion.

Grand Tour guests who opted to take a steamship named the *Zillah* boarded at the West Thumb docks. In 1903, passenger Hester Henshall wrote about her lake voyage, noting: "We stopped at Dot Island, a tiny green isle in the middle of the lake, on which are a number of animals, buffalo, elk, deer and antelope. They were fed with hay from the steamboat while we were there. The Captain warned us not to go near, as the big bull buffalo was very fierce. He finally did make a terrific rush and butted the fence until I feared the structure would go down before his fierce onslaughts. He was the last animal fed, and the Doctor [her husband, Dr. James Henshell] said that was the cause of his demonstration; that it was all for effect, and to get us aboard again as the Captain wanted to get the passengers to land at his curio store in season. The man brought another bale of hay and fed the big buffalo, who suddenly became very docile, and we left him quietly munching his hay. I guess the doctor was right."[12] *[Photo courtesy of the National Park Service, Yellowstone National Park YELL#163]*

The boat ride took several hours, and by 1896, included a stop at Dot Island, one of eight islands on Yellowstone Lake. Waters created a zoo of sorts on the island where guests could see wild animals up close. This sounds odd today, given the more than four thousand bison that roam Yellowstone, but in those days, the park held only about four hundred bison. (America's bison population, which once numbered in the hundreds of millions, had been decimated in the mid-1800s by hunters seeking fur, skin, and meat; by 1890, less than one thousand bison remained nationwide.)[14] Captain Waters actually bought four bison from famed Texas rancher Charles Goodnight (the inspiration for crusty Woodrow F. Call in Larry McMurtry's Pulitzer Prize–winning novel, *Lonesome Dove*) and had them shipped to Yellowstone.[15] The bison, elk, and pronghorn lived summers on Dot Island and winters in holding pens behind Waters' house, next to the Lake Hotel.

After a relaxing time on the lake, *Zillah* passengers arrived at a dock located in front of the Lake Hotel, just to the left of today's lake-viewing platform. From here, they walked up the short hill to the hotel and checked in for another fun night on their adventure.

The driver's motivation: a fifty-cents-a-head commission for every guest that opted for the *Zillah*. If all eleven passengers on board signed up, the driver received $5.50—around $143 in modern terms.[13] Years later, the *Zillah's* owner, Captain E. C. Waters, rescinded the commission, and drivers got even, badmouthing the steamer as unreliable. More guests continued on by stagecoach, which proved a bad deal, since sandy ground plagued the nineteen miles between West Thumb and the Lake Hotel. Passengers sometimes had to get out and walk.

About the *Zillah*...

- **Built:** 1884, in Dubuque, Iowa, by Captain William McCrory

- **Construction:** 81 feet by 14 feet; 40 tons; steel hull; screw propeller

- **Passenger capacity:** 125

- **Cost:** $20,000, purchased by the Yellowstone Park Association in 1890, the same year that Captain E. C. Waters was awarded a concessions contract to operate his Yellowstone Lake Boat Company. By 1897, Waters owned the *Zillah* outright.

- **How the boat got to Yellowstone:** Transported by rail in sections from Lake Minnetonka, Minnesota, to Cinnabar, Montana, and then taken by horse-drawn wagons to the Lake Outlet. As reported in the April 27, 1891, edition of *The Helena Independent:* "It was a big undertaking and necessitated an enormous outlay of money. The boiler alone weighed six tons or over, and required twenty mules to pull it from Cinnabar to the lake."[16]

- **Named for:** *Zillah* is a Biblical name that means "protection." But most likely, Waters chose to name his steamship after Zillah Oakes, daughter of Thomas F. Oakes, president of the Northern Pacific Railroad from 1888 to 1893.

- **Reputation:** Acting Superintendent George Anderson noted in his 1892 report: "The steamer on the lake has been running successfully for a year or more and adds much to the pleasure of a trip through the park. It is commodious and comfortable, and I believe perfectly safe."[17]

- **Fate:** Taken out of service in 1907, when Waters lost his boat company lease. The hull is believed to have been sunk in the lake.

The *Zillah* plies Yellowstone Lake. *[Photo courtesy of the National Park Service.]*

The Legacy of E. C. Waters

In the early years of the Lake Hotel's history, nobody stands out more than a colorful character named Ela Collins Waters, better known as E. C. Waters.

Waters came to Yellowstone in the mid-1880s, and in 1887, became the general manager in charge of hotels for the park's governing entity, the Yellowstone Park Association. He later helped oversee construction of the Lake Hotel, and made so many mistakes, it helped cost him his job. He quickly rebounded, though, snagging Yellowstone's first-ever boat business. Between 1891 and 1907, Captain Waters ferried thousands of passengers between West Thumb and the Lake Hotel on his steamboat, the *Zillah*.

In the *Zillah's* early years, park military officials had nothing but nice things to say in their annual reports about Waters and his steamboat. Complaints came from guests renting private boats and fishing tackle, who considered Waters' rates inflated.

As the years went by, Captain Waters acquired more critics. Then, in 1905, he commissioned the construction of another boat—one that would help lead to his undoing. Anxious about possible competition on the lake, Waters spent $60,000 (about $1.5 million in today's dollars) for a 500-passenger steamship, which he humbly named the *E. C. Waters*. But his unpopularity made it difficult for him to license the boat (among other issues), so the *E. C. Waters* mostly just sat at the dock.

However, the fatal blow to Waters and his

Left: Captain Ela C. Waters [Photo courtesy of the National Park Service]

Above: The irascible E. C. Waters struts out on the Lake Hotel dock, next to his elk-antler-adorned steamer, the *Zillah*. Waters built the house (shown in the background) for his wife and children; the Lake Hotel roofline can be seen through the trees to the left. [Photo courtesy of the Montana Historical Society Research Center]

8396. Steamboat on Lake, Yellowstone National Park.

Guests board the *E. C. Waters*, a 140-foot by 30-foot wooden-hulled steamship, which often sat at the Lake Hotel dock. *[Photo courtesy of the National Park Service, Yellowstone National Park YELL# 29085]*

Yellowstone tenure involved his alleged neglect of animals on Dot Island. By 1907, when the boat company lease was up for renewal, the government not only refused to renew it, Park Superintendent Samuel Young declared that "E. C. Waters, president of the Yellowstone Lake Boat Company, having rendered himself obnoxious during the season of 1907, is...debarred from the park and will not be allowed to return without permission."[18]

Eventually, the captain left the park—but he left a big piece of himself behind. Today, if you take the summer scenic cruise out of Bridge Bay Marina, you'll circle Stevenson Island (the big island directly in front of the Lake Hotel) and see the spine of an old ship unfurled in shallow waters. This is what's left of the *E. C. Waters*. When Waters was forced out of business, he moored the boat in a sheltered cove on Stevenson Island, where it sat until 1921, when east winds blew it ashore. Here it remained, listing, until five years later, when park officials cut two holes in the hull and removed the steamer's two boilers for use at the Lake Hotel.

Then, in 1930, the unthinkable happened—at least in terms of historic preservation. Spurred by a park edict to spruce things up, rangers burned the *E. C. Waters*, leaving behind its spiny skeleton.

Waters lived his final years in the Old Soldiers Home in Fond du Lac, Wisconsin (the city where he grew up), and died in 1926. But his name lives on each summer, repeated daily by scenic-cruise guides as the Lake Queen glides past the eerie remnants of the *E. C. Waters*.

After the *E. C. Waters* blew ashore on Stevenson Island, its listing hulk became a cold-weather warming hut for guests skiing on the frozen lake, and a summer playhouse for employees, like this group pictured in 1923. *[Photo courtesy of Randy Ingersoll]*

The spine of the *E. C. Waters* is all that remains on Stevenson Island. *[Photo courtesy of the National Park Service]*

Fourth Night: The Lovely Lake Hotel

The Lake Hotel, as simple as it looked the first twelve years of its existence, had to excite guests, whether they arrived by stagecoach or steamer. In those days, heavy timber surrounded the hotel, giving it a frontier appearance, which appealed to big-city travelers intent on having a Buffalo Bill adventure.

The Lake Hotel, like the Fountain Hotel, offered steam heat and electricity, and many of the amenities of modern lodging. According to an 1891 Yellowstone Park Association price guide, ladies could have their plain dresses steam cleaned for twenty-five cents to fifty cents, and their "fancy" dresses for fifty cents to three dollars. For men, seventy-five cents spiffed up a vest, pair of pants, and coat. Cigars ranged in price from twelve and a half cents for a "No. 4" to twenty-five cents for a

"No. 1," and an entire box of No. 4s could be had for three bucks.[19]

Some of the hotel's other offerings: a Western Union telegram could be sent for twenty cents. A shave cost twenty-five cents; a haircut, fifty cents; and boot blacking, ten cents a pair. Two bits (twenty-five cents) bought a bath—important since none of the original rooms at the Lake Hotel had private bathrooms.[20]

In 1891, most guests traveled as part of a prepaid tour, but those who came on their own paid $4 a night (about $104 in today's dollars). Those that stayed longer than six nights paid only $3 a night.

Anything French was in vogue during this Belle Époque era, so guests had their choice of many foreign vintages of wine. Indeed, dining was an impressive affair, with white linen tablecloths, delicate china, heavy silverware, and fresh wildflower arrangements that the all-female

Left: Victorian Clothing [Photos courtesy of OldDesignShop.com]

Above: This photo of bears eating kitchen scraps was shot behind the Lake Hotel. Recalling his 1903 Grand Tour stay at the Lake Hotel, Stephen M. Dale wrote, "The bears learn to expect their dinner, and the people learn to expect the bears; and neither one is ever disappointed. That evening, we counted twelve [bears] and went close enough to them to take pictures."[21] [Photo courtesy of the National Park Service, Yellowstone National Park YELL#129908]

Opposite: Many guests loved fishing for cutthroat trout on Yellowstone Lake; if they caught anything, the kitchen chefs would cook the trout for a small fee (which is still true today). Fresh-caught fish often graced the hotel menus as well. [Photo courtesy of the National Park Service, Yellowstone National Park YELL#43576]

waitstaff picked from the hotel grounds.

Chefs at the Lake Hotel prepared elegant meals on a twelve-foot-long, three-hole range made by Bramhall, Deane & Co. that originally burned hard (high-quality) coal before being converted to burn wood. The kitchen's "Minnesota-style" refrigerator, which measured an immense thirteen feet by six feet by twelve feet, cost $200, and was manufactured by the Minnesota Refrigerator Company. Other appliances included a twenty-four-inch broiler and a fifteen-gallon coffee urn, both made by Wolterstorff, Moritz & Co., in St. Paul, Minnesota.[22]

Fortunately, by that point in history, electricity lit many American cities and the Lake Hotel too. In the hotel's engine room, an Edison Dynamo 120-light generator provided the juice that brightened the rooms.

As comfortable as the Lake Hotel may have been, it was not the area's main draw. Guests fished the lake, which teamed with cutthroat trout, and they trooped behind the hotel nightly to watch bears feast on kitchen scraps. Sometimes, they just sat on the front porch or upstairs on the veranda, absorbing the surrounding beauty.

Last Stop: The Canyon Hotel

After a relaxing night at the Lake Hotel, guests again boarded the coaches and headed up the park's east side to the Grand Canyon of the Yellowstone. Along the way, they passed the Mud Volcano and the magnificent Hayden Valley, where—if fortunate—they spied bison, elk, or even wolves. (It wasn't until 1915 that an all-out effort began to eradicate wolves, considered at the time to be detrimental—a task completed by 1925. Wolves, now considered beneficial to Yellowstone's ecosystem, were reintroduced in 1995). Coaches arrived at the Canyon Hotel in time for lunch, which left the afternoon free for guests to explore.

The Canyon Hotel *[Photo courtesy of the National Park Service]*

Most guests wanted to view the canyon's Upper and Lower Falls, or ride on horseback along an eight-mile trail that meandered through pines along the canyon rim.

But the more adventurous longed to climb down into the vast ravine. Today, anybody with the strength to walk down 328 steps and back up again—the rough equivalent of a twenty-story building—can tackle Uncle Tom's Trail. The reward: an up-close peek at the 308-foot, cascading Lower Falls. Back then, though, the trail didn't have steps; travelers (including women in long dresses) used ropes and ladders to make the descent.

A Bozeman, Montana, businessman named H. F. Richardson (nicknamed "Uncle Tom" by friends) created the trail in 1898 and led guests on the strenuous tour. "It was a pretty difficult climb for most people," Yellowstone Historian Lee Whittlesey told the *Bozeman Daily Chronicle.* "He would bring pins for the ladies to pin up their dresses to make the hiking easier."[23] Richardson's business thrived until 1905, when a wooden staircase replaced the original trail.

The Canyon Hotel opened in 1890 and provided adequate lodging on the Grand Tour. Some described the hotel as "barn like," while others, like Superintendent F. A. Boutelle, simply called it "an unsightly affair." Boutelle, though, also wrote that the hotel would "be a very comfortable and commodious house."[24] In 1911, architect Robert Reamer built a much more spectacular Canyon Hotel, but this hotel—like the Fountain—met an untimely demise: closed because the shifting ground caused structural cracks, it mysteriously burned to the ground in 1960.

The early Canyon Hotel may not have wowed guests, but the Grand Canyon did. The Grand Canyon of the Yellowstone was considered the Grand Tour's premiere attraction—a bigger wow than even the Old Faithful Geyser (which is why it was saved for last).

Finally, on their last morning, guests boarded the bright-yellow Observation Wagons and rolled across the park's center to Norris for lunch. Then, perhaps a touch wistfully, they returned to the National Hotel in Mammoth Hot Springs for a farewell dinner. After more than five days of travel and adventure, the time had come to return to reality.

To bid *adieu* to Wonderland.

The Uncle Tom's Trail excursion included a boat trip across the Yellowstone River and a campfire supper in the woods. *[Photo courtesy of the National Park Service]*

By the early 1900s, Yellowstone had swelled in popularity, and lodging like the Lake Hotel either needed updating or replacing.

It was a time of prosperity for wealthy Americans—of "anything's possible." Titans like Cornelius Vanderbilt, with his railroads; John D. Rockefeller, with his oil; and Andrew Carnegie, with his steel, had earned millions, and altered the country's psyche in the process.

The automobile allowed people to go places they had never been before, including the once faraway west. It would be 1915 before Yellowstone admitted the first car, but that didn't stop Americans from coming by train. The park now attracted an emerging middle class anxious to see exploding geysers and wild animals.

It would prove to be a time of metamorphosis for Yellowstone— especially for the Lake Hotel, which would emerge from its humble cocoon to become a majestic butterfly.

Harry Child Finds His Man

In 1903, a Montana banker named Harry Child ran the show in Yellowstone. Child ruled the park's two major concessionaires: the Yellowstone Park Association, which owned all park lodging, and the Yellowstone Transportation Company, the park's number-

one provider of stagecoach and horse-pulled transportation.

Twelve years had passed since the opening of the Fountain Hotel in the Lower Geyser Basin, the Canyon Hotel in the Grand Canyon of the Yellowstone, and the Lake Hotel at the Lake Outlet. So when the national government pressed for better hotels, Child responded by securing a dynamic, new breed of architect.

Child's quest took him to the Hotel del Coronado in San Diego, where his friend Elisha S. Babcock was the manager. Child had a winter home in nearby La Jolla, California, and was familiar with the upscale hotel. The "Del," as regulars called it, opened in 1888 and had become a West Coast favorite for the country's elite. Getting there required a week-long train ride from the East Coast, but the rich traveled in their own personal train cars, which they stored on side tracks at the Del. The Queen Anne–style hotel even ran a school for the children of wealthy long-term travelers.

It is here, at this hotel of grandeur, that Child and Robert Reamer first met. Reamer, a young, promising architect, came with kudos for his recent renovation work on the Del, and his design of the nearby Coronado Tent City. The striped tents provided a growing middle class with an affordable way to vacation on the seashore. Reamer had also designed a music and dance pavilion for Tent City, and remodeled the Coronado Golf Club House—which Child openly admired.

Opposite: Robert Reamer's 1903–04 renovation included construction of a wooden veranda that graced the full front length of the hotel—adding a touch of Grand Hotel distinction.
[Photo courtesy of the Montana Historical Society Research Center]

Harry Child—who, along with his family, ruled most Yellowstone concessions from the early 1900s until 1966—somehow convinced Robert Reamer to leave metropolitan San Diego and come to rugged Yellowstone to design his hotels. *[Photo courtesy of the National Park Service]*

After Child hired him, twenty-nine-year-old Reamer quickly packed his bags and moved to Yellowstone, where he would return again and again, completing more than forty projects in the park through the course of his life.

Child could not have been more pleased. He had found the right man for the job—the architectural genius who would create hotels and other buildings never before imagined in Yellowstone.

Visionary Robert Reamer

When Robert Reamer arrived in Yellowstone in 1903, he hit the ground running, simultaneously tackling two major hotel projects: the construction of the Old Faithful Inn and the transformation of the Lake Hotel.

The projects could not have been more different. At Old Faithful, a full day's buggy ride from the Lake Hotel, he created something quite new—a giant, storybook log cabin flanking the world's most famous geyser. And at the Lake Hotel, he took something rough and blasé, and molded it into something that the rich recognized and loved.

Reamer had never attempted such large projects before, but his life's path had prepared him. In her richly detailed book, *Weaver of Dreams: The Life and Architecture of Robert C. Reamer,* author Ruth Quinn explains that Yellowstone's premiere architect grew up in Oberlin, Ohio, but moved to Detroit at age twelve to live with relatives. Though quite young, he managed to secure a job working as a draftsman in an architect's office—a launch pad for his future career.[1]

By 1890, the same year that the Lake Hotel was in the throes of its initial construction, Reamer had moved to Chicago, where he worked as a designer for a furniture-manufacturing firm. Interestingly, his company, A. H. Andrews & Co., was among the exhibitors in the Manufacturers and Liberal Arts Building at the 1893 World's Columbian Exposition.[2] The Chicago fair featured more than two hundred buildings of predominately neoclassic architecture, sparking a revival in Colonial architecture. Likely, Reamer attended that fair and absorbed everything he saw, including the "look" that would inspire the Lake Hotel's Colonial turnaround ten years later.

By 1895, Reamer was in San Diego and making a name for himself as a young architect. He and partner Samuel Zimmer opened an architectural firm—Zimmer & Reamer—where Reamer sharpened his skills designing homes and commercial buildings.[3] His work with the Hotel del Coronado, though, would be his turning point—his fateful leap from ordinary to extraordinary.

Robert Reamer *[Photo courtesy of the National Park Service]*

785 – TENT CITY, CORONADO, CALIFORNIA.

At Tent City on Coronado Island, a fully furnished, striped-canvas tent for two ran $6 per week; electricity cost an additional $1 per month. *[Photo courtesy of the author's collection]*

7528. Grand Hotel, Mackinac Island, Mich.

Architect Robert Reamer realized that upscale Lake Hotel guests would feel more comfortable in a hotel that resembled neoclassic East Coast resorts like the Grand Hotel on Mackinac Island in Michigan, which still survives today. *[Photo courtesy of the author's collection]*

Reamer had his hands full when he arrived in Yellowstone in the winter of 1903. That year, beyond working on the two hotel projects, he also designed the Northern Pacific Railway passenger station in Gardiner, Montana (razed in 1954); the West Thumb Lunch Station (razed in 1927); the Commissary Building in Mammoth Hot Springs (razed in 1937); the W. A. Hall Store in Gardiner (still standing); and an addition to the Klamer Store in the Upper Geyser Basin (now a Yellowstone General Store operated by Delaware North). In addition, Reamer designed the Transportation Building in Mammoth, which originally housed horses, stagecoaches, and surreys, and later, the park's large fleet of transportation vehicles.[4] It tragically burned in 1925, destroying ninety-three trucks and vehicles.

The two hotels, though, brought Reamer the bulk of his early fame. Oddly, when finished, the Lake Hotel received the most applause for its style, while the Old Faithful Inn raised eyebrows with its then-unusual rustic design. Now, opinion has flopped. The Inn has become the iconic national-park hotel, and the Lake Hotel gets quizzical stares—mostly for its yellow color, which some consider glaring and unnatural in the forest setting.

In 1904, though, guests staying at the newly renovated Lake Hotel must have been delighted to discover a Colonial-themed hotel—so unexpected and so elegant on the shores of Yellowstone Lake.

The Long-Lost Ell

When architect Robert Reamer began renovations on the Lake Hotel, he intended to build the long east wing that exists today. But Reamer hit a snag named Captain Ela C. Waters, whose home and boat business occupied leased land east of the original hotel. Park President Harry Child assumed that Waters would be reasonable and move his animal pens (which guests found smelly), but Waters refused.

So Reamer did the next best thing, building the hotel's mid-section, and then literally turning the corner to add a north-jutting wing known as the "ell." The ell wing connected to the hotel where the staircase by the deli is located today.

Reamer's renovation cost $79,202, or around $2.1 million in today's dollars,[5] and it bumped the room count up to 210—enough to accommodate 466 people. The Lake Hotel then offered the largest number of guest rooms in Yellowstone.

Harry Child had to be a happy man.

The ell wing, which extended into the land occupied by today's parking lot, was torn down in 1940—a shame since the Lake Hotel sells out nightly in the summer. *[Photo courtesy of the National Park Service, Yellowstone National Park YELL#30201]*

The Lady Gets a Facelift

When Robert Reamer began the expansion of the Lake Hotel, he obviously realized that the hotel's original bones could shoulder a neoclassic transformation. His design choice also had merit, given that the Colonial look was in the midst of an architectural revival.

And so it began, this transformation of a backwoods-simple hotel into something lakefront special: a sprawling affair featuring pillar-supported porticos, false balconies, dormers, and an array of whimsical windows. *[Photos courtesy of Joshua D. Stein]*

Twelve fifty-foot-tall Roman Ionic columns support the hotel's three monumental porticoes. The fluted shaft columns, made of wood, were constructed in Chicago, shipped by rail to Gardiner, Montana, and brought to the Lake Hotel by wagon.

Reamer embedded six small dormers—three on each side of the center portico—in the hotel roof. The dormers mirror the three porticoes in design.

The fifteen false balconies that dress the front of the hotel's third-floor windows enhance its neoclassic persona. Reamer changed the original four-over-four, double-sash windows to eighteen-over-eighteen panes—again, for Colonial Revival effect.

Lunette, or half-moon, windows adorn the triangular faces of the east and west porticoes. Each lunette features eight-section fanlight sashes.

The full entablatures of the projecting porticoes include three-step architraves crowned by leaf-and-dart ogee moldings, plain friezes, and cornices elaborated with crown moldings.

Guests love what they call the "spider web" windows, technically known as oculus windows, popular in neoclassic-revival architecture.

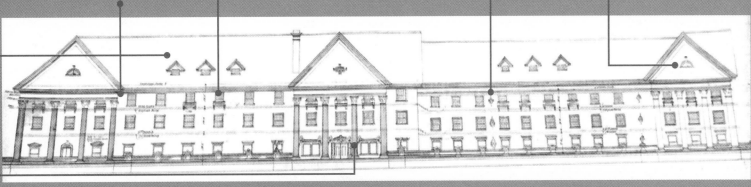

This 1903 blueprint shows Robert Reamer's vision of the Lake Hotel's exterior. *[Photo courtesy of the National Park Service, Yellowstone National Park Archives]*

A California-Redwood Lobby

Robert Reamer not only updated the hotel's exterior, he brought an entirely new look to the interior. He started by eliminating several 1891-era rooms in the lobby area.

Next, Reamer enriched the lobby walls, columns, and ceiling beams with California redwood. This new Lake Hotel lobby exuded a man's man persona, with an abundance of straight-back chairs and rockers, an assortment of leather-top tables, and a smattering of well-placed spittoons. Reamer also realigned the lobby's Queen Anne–style staircase so that guests ascended south to north (today's alignment), instead of the original west to east.

Then Reamer flexed his architectural muscles, building the hotel's center wing, where today's ground-floor restrooms and deli reside. The hotel's original blueprint shows that this wing was planned for construction in 1891, but it was delayed because of time constraints and other construction issues. Once completed, the wing held rooms and communal bathrooms on all three floors.

The hotel had expanded—but Reamer was not done.

This picture of the renovated 1904 lobby was taken in the area near today's dining room, looking toward the registration desk. *[Photo courtesy of the National Park Service, Yellowstone National Park YELL#128]*

The Grand Lady Makes Her Debut

Construction of the new and improved Lake Hotel spanned 1903 and 1904, with Reamer on-site only part of the time; he was stretched thin with multiple projects going on simultaneously in the park. Compared to the hotel's original construction in 1890, this project went considerably smoother. Supplies still came by freight wagon, but the roads had improved; and park leaders did a better job of keeping work on track.

When finished, the visual effect was stunning—and name changing. Postcards of that day show that the hotel became known as the Lake Colonial Hotel, the Colonial Lake Hotel, or simply as the Colonial Hotel. The "Colonial" reference stuck until after World War I.

The timing of the hotel's new look could not have been better. It epitomized the Golden Era of grand hotels, with its wood-frame construction, clapboard siding, countless windows, and multiple entrances. It gave guests a taste of the unexpected yet provided a grounded feeling of the familiar, exuding an East Coast persona in a Wild West setting.

Author Reau Campbell, in his 1913 Yellowstone guidebook, summed up the hotel this way: "The Colonial is a splendid, modern hotel, with the woods on each side and the back of it, and the most beautiful lake in the world in front of it; and within its doors, every comfort to be desired and good living withal. Oh! This is a good place to stop, to rest from your journey and from wonder seeing, and to prepare for the scenic grandeur to come when you start out again."[6]

Between 1904 and 1915, the Lake Hotel nestled into the most genteel years of its existence, offering fine lodging, wonderful food and wines, and a plethora of outdoor experiences. Architect Robert Reamer doubled the size of the dining room in 1912, but otherwise, the hotel just hummed along.

In 1915, however, the automobile entered Yellowstone, and the slower, serene days of stagecoach travel came to a hoof-screeching halt.

Model Ts quickly became regular fixtures on American roads in the early 1900s, but not in Yellowstone. The biggest reason: concessionaires like Park President Harry Child had big money invested in horses and coaches.

"Possibly a thousand rigs ranging from the big Tally-Hos down to [the] two-horse surreys, and as many as two thousand horses, were in use at the top of the seasons from 1890 until 1915," writes historian Richard A. Bartlett in *Yellowstone: A Wilderness Besieged.*[1]

But Yellowstone officials could only stall the automobile's entry for so long. Cars had already driven into every other national park then in existence: Wind Cave in 1903, Mount Rainier in 1908, Crater Lake in 1911, Glacier in 1912, Yosemite and Sequoia in 1913, Mesa Verde in 1914, and Rocky Mountain in 1915.[2]

Finally, the old way of doing things ran out of gas. Privately owned automobiles legally entered Yellowstone on August 1, 1915—and nothing was ever the same again.

Coaches Versus Autos

The summer of 1916 must have been kind of crazy in Yellowstone, when the now-legal automobile and the yet-to-be-phased-out stagecoach shared park roads. The big problem: Cars backfired, horses spooked—and sometimes they bolted.

Park leaders solved the problem by creating a staggered schedule that put cars and coaches on the roads at different times of the day. For instance, a car-driving guest headed from the Lake Hotel to the Canyon Hotel had two options: (1) leave the Lake between 7:00 and 7:30 AM and arrive at the Canyon Hotel no earlier than 9:30 AM and no later than 10:10 AM, or (2) leave the Lake between 2:00 and 2:30 PM and arrive at the Canyon between 3:15 and 3:45 PM.[3]

Drivers who arrived early or late faced penalties—and the possibility of encountering a horse-drawn vehicle on the road. The fine: 50 cents per minute for the first five minutes late; $1 per minute for the next twenty minutes. Those who arrived early could be fined $25 or ejected from the park. And the park superintendent might impose both penalties if the guest arrived more than twenty-five minutes early![4]

Opposite: After the automobile entered Yellowstone in 1915, the park began the process of selling its stagecoaches and investing in touring cars. Pictured here is one of the park's first touring cars, manufactured by the White Motor Company of Cleveland, Ohio. The cars got bigger and better over the years, and eventually evolved into the Historic Yellow Buses we know today. *[Photo courtesy of the National Park Service, Yellowstone National Park YELL#200806]*

Yellowstone touring cars pull away from the Lake Hotel in 1917—the park's first full summer season without stagecoaches. Also interesting about this image is the large house shown at right. It belonged to the legendary, controversial, Captain E. C. Waters, who had the house built for his family in 1890; they moved out after 1907, when Waters was banished from the park. The large, rambling house stood until 1922, when it was razed for construction of the hotel's east wing. *[Photo courtesy of the Montana Historical Society Research Center]*

Mission Style Furniture

By 1917, the straight-back chairs that dominated the 1904 lobby had mostly been replaced by Mission style rockers and chairs that complemented existing leather-topped tables. It's possible this furniture came from the 1890-opened Canyon Hotel, given that Robert Reamer built a new Canyon Hotel in 1911 and it featured wicker furniture. The old furniture had to go somewhere—possibly the Lake Hotel.

AUTOMOBILE RESERVATION

_____191_

YELLOWSTONE PARK HOTEL CO.
Yellowstone Park, Wyoming

Gentlemen:
I will enter the Park on _____
via _____ Entrance.
I expect to spend _____ days in the Park.
The members of my party and accommodations required are as follows:

NAME	ROOMS

Yours truly,

NOTE: Rates—American Plan only:
Board and Room, regular accommodations...........$5.00 per day each
Board and Room, choice location, including bath—one person ....$7.00 per day each
Board and Room, ditto, two persons...........$6.50 per day each
Board and Room, ditto, three or more persons...........$6.00 per day each

Above: In the automobile's earliest days, guests filled out an automobile reservation form that detailed their upcoming Yellowstone itinerary. "My dear Motorist," Huntley Child (son of Park President Harry Child) wrote potential guests on June 5, 1916. "Of course you will motor to Yellowstone Park this summer. Write to us concerning the details of your trip; tell us how many there will be in your party, by which entrance you will come, and what hotel accommodations you will require. A blank [form] is enclosed for this information."[5] _[Photo courtesy of the National Park Service, Yellowstone National Park Archives]_

Right: In 1917, guests entered the hotel through the double doors shown at left and registered at a desk located just to the right of the staircase. The wooden counter pictured on the lobby's north wall (where today's fireplace sits) served as a curio shop. _[Photo courtesy of the Montana Historical Society Research Center]_

Boating at the Lake Hotel

Boating on Yellowstone Lake had to be among life's greatest pleasures while visiting the Lake Hotel. Lucky for guests, the docks bobbed an easy two-minute stroll away from the hotel's front door.

The history of the docks begins with Captain E. C. Waters, who in 1890 secured the first-ever boat business lease on Yellowstone Lake. Guests visited his on-site store—located next door to the hotel—to secure a lake excursion, a boat rental or to obtain fishing tackle. In 1907, after Captain Waters so annoyed park leaders that they kicked him out of Yellowstone, a sportsman named T. E. Hofer bought the business and renamed it the T. E. Hofer Boat Company. Three years later, he bought a steamer named the *Jean D*, which enabled guests on the Grand Tour to once again cruise between West Thumb and the Lake Hotel—rather than travel to the Lake by dusty stagecoach.

Hofer had made a name for himself as an animal hunter for the Smithsonian Institute, but he apparently lacked business skills. By 1911, he was ready to sell, and Park President Harry Child—always looking to expand his empire—was ready to buy. The newly named Yellowstone Park Boat Company now ruled Yellowstone Lake, offering guests an assortment of rentals, including motorboats, rowboats, and dories.

The Lake Hotel docks existed until 1963, when they were moved to the newly built, wind-protected Bridge Bay Marina, located two miles west of the Lake Hotel. Though the Lake site was convenient for guests, high winds and waves frequently battered the marina, causing boats to be cast adrift—or worse, sunk.

Above: The *Jean D* became the flagship steamer of the Lake Hotel marina in 1910, replacing the retired *Zillah*. *[Photo courtesy of the National Park Service, Yellowstone National Park YELL#192534]* Right: Fishing has long been a favored pastime on Yellowstone Lake. *[Photo courtesy of National Park Service, Yellowstone National Park YELL#43549]*

A Little About the Big Lake

- **Elevation:** 7,733 feet, making it the largest fresh water lake at this elevation in North America

- **Surface Area:** 131.7 square miles, or 88,000 acres

- **Shoreline:** 141 miles

- **Compass Miles:** Twenty miles north to south; fourteen miles east to west

- **Average Depth:** 140 feet

- **Maximum Depth:** 410 feet

- **Average Water Temperature:** 42 degrees

- **Winter Ice:** The lake typically freezes in early December, and defrosts in late May or early June. Ice thickens two to three feet, except over the lake's thermal features.

- **Types of Fish:** Yellowstone cutthroat trout, longnose dace, redside shiners, longnose suckers, and lake chubs. In 1994, a species known as lake trout were discovered in Yellowstone Lake, and efforts have since focused on their removal (they eat cutthroat trout, and have decimated the population). The cutthroat is now endangered and illegal to keep; however, lake trout MUST be kept or killed if caught.

- **Deaths:** Yellowstone Lake, calm in the morning, can become ocean-like in the afternoon. Boats have many times capsized in the six-foot swells. Lee Whittlesey, author of *Death in Yellowstone*, writes that the lake has claimed the lives of more than one hundred people, usually because of hypothermia, which starts to set in fifteen minutes after a person falls in the water. In comparison, as of 2015, bears have killed just nine people since the park's formation in 1872.

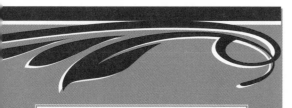

Here's a look at the prices guests paid in 1912 for boats and fishing tackle at the Lake Hotel dock (under Harry Child's management):

- Round-trip excursion on the *Jean D* from the Lake Hotel to West Thumb: $5 ($121 in today's dollars)

- *Jean D* excursion to the southeast arm of Yellowstone Lake: $2 per person with a ten-person minimum ($48 per person today)

- Rental of the *Jean D* for the entire day: $35 ($845 today)

- Powerboat rental: $3 per hour ($72 today)

- Hired oarsman: 50 cents per hour ($12 today)

- Rod, reel, line, and landing net rental: 50 cents per hour ($12 today)

- Fishing flies: 5 to 25 cents each ($1.21 to $6.04 today)[6]

1918: Hello, National Park Service (Goodbye, U.S. Army)

In terms of historical significance, the year 1916 was huge in Yellowstone. Not only had the automobile finally inched its way into the park the year before, but Congress passed the National Park Service Organic Act, creating the National Park Service (NPS).

This meant a major change for Yellowstone, which had been under the protective rule of the U.S. Army since 1886. The army, which was based at Fort Yellowstone in Mammoth Hot Springs, kept a sharp eye on the park's 2.2 million acres—especially in the early years, when poachers threatened bison and other resident critters.

By 1916, though, the country had ten national parks and twenty national monuments, all of which required supervision and protection. This is where Stephen T. Mather entered the picture.

Mather was a self-made millionaire who co-owned Thorkildsen-Mather Borax Company. In 1912, he met environmentalist John Muir on a hike in California's Sequoia National Park—and it changed his life. In coming years, Mather used much of his own money to crusade for the creation of a federal agency that would oversee the country's national parks. For his efforts, Mather in 1916 was named the first director of the newly formed NPS.

Unfortunately, Mather suffered occasional bouts of severe depression and was hospitalized when the NPS became a reality. Horace Albright,

Industrialist Stephen Mather campaigned hard for the creation of a unified federal agency to oversee the administration of the national parks. The National Park Service will celebrate its 100th anniversary in 2016. *[Photo courtesy of the National Park Service]*

who served as Mather's secretary, stepped in as acting director to organize the new bureau, establish policies and procedures, and lobby Congress for money to run the fledgling organization. Indeed, the NPS could not truly begin its Yellowstone legacy until Congress provided the necessary funding. Finally, in October 1918, the NPS officially took over, and the army—after thirty-two years of protecting America's first national park—left Fort Yellowstone.

The year 1918 also proved significant for the Lake Hotel. With most of the hotel's male staff off fighting the war—and with a slew of wartime restrictions in place—the hotel shut down for the summer season and stayed closed until the summer of 1920.

Here, in 1915, U.S. Army soldiers practice with a machine gun, presumably at Fort Yellowstone in Mammoth Hot Springs. World War I had ignited the year before, but the United States didn't enter the conflict until 1917—which affected staffing at the Lake Hotel. *[Photo courtesy of the National Park Service]*

Learn more about the work of Stephen Mather and Horace Albright, along with the entire history of national parks and monuments, by watching the wonderful six-part documentary by Ken Burns, *The National Parks: America's Best Idea.*[7]

A New *Porte Cochére* Ushers in Roaring 1920s

The Lake Hotel closed in 1918 and 1919 because of World War I, and park leaders used the down time to make improvements. In front of the hotel's center columns, a *porte cochére* (covered drive-through) emerged, built so guests could enter and exit their cars without worry of weather.

Also, concrete replaced the quaint wooden porch that ran the entire length of the hotel's front—an improvement that guests (wishing to sit outside and absorb the lake) still mourn today.

In 1920, the bloody war over, guests returned in droves, and the hotel carried on—ushering in a decade of significant change for the Lake Hotel.

Seemingly, the hotel roared along, just like the 1920s.

Guests congregate beneath the *porte cochére*, awaiting transportation to their next destination in this 1925 image. Look closely, and see the white caps of two maids peeking out from a third-floor window. *[Photo courtesy of the Montana Historical Society Research Center]*

ammers pounded at the Lake Hotel in the 1920s—but not continuously. The first growth spurt spanned the years, 1922–1924. The final work climaxed between 1928 and 1929.

Architect Robert Reamer outdid himself during the early years, designing the east wing; installing the Arts and Crafts–style fireplace; and feminizing the dark, masculine lobby. Then he returned for a swan song in 1928, building the north wing (that would eventually become today's gift shop) and creating the hotel's *pièce de résistance*—the signature sunroom.

The hotel had so many projects going on between 1922 and 1925 that another architectural firm was hired to help shoulder the load. Link & Haire (John Gustave Link and Charles S. Haire) of Helena, Montana, built a new female dormitory (now the Sandpiper Lodge), doubled the size of the dining room, and erected a Presidential Suite on the second floor. The duo also turned the ground-floor hallway, once filled with guestrooms, into a guest-friendly corridor that connected the east wing lobby with the main lobby.

When the hammers finally stopped swinging in 1929, the Grand Lady was finally done.

The Flat-Roofed East Wing

In 1922, when park leaders turned to Robert Reamer to work his magic on multiple projects at the Lake Hotel, the architect first tackled the east wing that he had intended to build in 1903.

Architecture, ever evolving, had changed since Reamer first gave the Lake Hotel its neoclassical design. In the early 1920s, leaner, cleaner lines dominated building trends, and Reamer, who reveled in mixing styles, embraced this new look. Today, the Lake Hotel truly is a potpourri of architecture and design trends—mostly because of the creative Reamer. The central staircase is part Colonial, part Victorian; the Batchelder fireplace is Arts and Crafts; the clapboard exterior is Colonial Revival.

When it was finished, the east wing offered 113 rooms and fifty-nine baths (every two rooms shared a bath—which was revolutionary at the Lake Hotel, where communal bathrooms still dominated). Guests appreciated the new rooms, but some have since questioned the wing's design. The long, flat roof does not match the rest of the pitched-roof hotel. And the front-porch portico seems too small and slightly forgotten compared to the twelve massive, ionic pillars that command the hotel's central section. Some guests, in fact, have disliked the wing so much they advocate

---

Opposite: In 1923, architect Robert Reamer dramatically altered the hotel's lobby, painting the redwood columns and paneling white, and replacing the dark Mission style furniture with Florida style wicker chairs and couches. Five years later, he also painted the ceiling beams white. [Photo courtesy of the National Park Service, Yellowstone National Park, YELL#94277]

tearing it down—something that hopefully will never happen.

Beyond its flat roof, the east wing has additional curiosities. The wing climbs in elevation, so the ground floor only has guest rooms halfway across. From the outside, though, it appears that the entire wing consists of four stories because Reamer installed windows on the ground floor where no rooms exist.

Above: With the completion of the east wing, the hotel spanned more than seven hundred feet and offered 323 rooms. Construction took two years and totaled $227,969 (or $3.2 million in today's dollars).[1] [Photo courtesy of Joshua D. Stein]

Right: This 1922 blueprint of the east wing shows how Robert Reamer built bathrooms in between rooms—a huge improvement over the chamber pots and the communal bathrooms down the hall that dominated the hotel up to this point. [Photo courtesy of the National Park Service, Yellowstone National Park Archives]

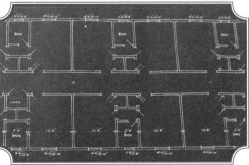

From Bat Alley to the Sandpiper

Back in the beginning of the Lake Hotel's existence, almost all employees lived somewhere in the hotel; dorms did not exist. Each of the hotel's three floors certainly housed a bellman and, no doubt, a maid, for middle-of-the-night emergencies.

Employees may have lived in the attic prior to Robert Reamer's 1903–04 renovation, but they certainly did thereafter. It was an all-female dorm occupied primarily by maids and waitresses. The dormer-window rooms (on the front side of the hotel) had to be envied, because they provided the best evening breeze in warm July and August.

These female employees had "wild" company in the attic too: bats—and bat droppings—earning the attic the nickname "Bat Alley."

So, the new two-story female dorm—the Sandpiper—was a welcome change when it was built in 1923. It rose behind the hotel, rather close to the east wing (which was simultaneously under construction), and featured fifty-seven bedrooms and a communal upstairs bathroom. Link & Haire designed the dorm, but it's

This photo shows the hotel rafters where employees once lived. The vertical paneling appears to be from the "bat alley" era, prior to 1923. [*Photo courtesy of the author*]

Here is the Sandpiper dorm, photographed in 1924, shortly after its completion. [*Photo courtesy of the National Park Service, Yellowstone National Park, YELL#29975-30262*]

Female residents obeyed an 11:00 PM curfew— or faced repercussions.

interesting to note how the dorm's flat-roof design resembles Robert Reamer's east wing.

The Sandpiper was at first a true woman's dorm. Gentleman callers were not allowed beyond the lobby, and female residents obeyed an 11:00 PM curfew—or faced repercussions from the dorm matron.

The dorm went coed in the early 1980s, which led to free-spirited employees playing their boom boxes too loud and disturbing hotel residents.

That's when new dorms sprang up nearby, and the Sandpiper was renovated (every room received a private bathroom) and renamed the Annex, providing overflow lodging for hotel guests.

During the hotel's 2014 renovation, the Annex received a familiar new name: the Sandpiper Lodge. And in the winter of 2015, the former dorm received a major makeover, bringing it on par with its elegant mother ship.

The Long Yellow Hotel

- **Hotel Length:** 720 feet, or 240 yards. It's twice the length of a National Football League field.

- **Longest Wooden Hotel—Not:** It's been boasted as the longest existing wooden hotel in the world, but that's not true. For instance, the wooden Grand Hotel on Michigan's Mackinac Island stretches nine hundred feet.

- **Clapboard Siding:** Mostly pine, harvested from nearby forests in 1890, 1903 and 1922. A temporary sawmill set up on site cut the boards.

- **Paint:** Custom color, Yellowstone Lake Colonial Yellow by Sherwin Williams. The actual shade and brand of yellow has shifted over the years.

- **Gallons Needed:** It takes one coat of primer and two coats of yellow paint—or about 3,500 gallons—to cover the exterior.

- **Cost per Gallon:** About $30. Total cost for yellow exterior: around $105,000.[2]

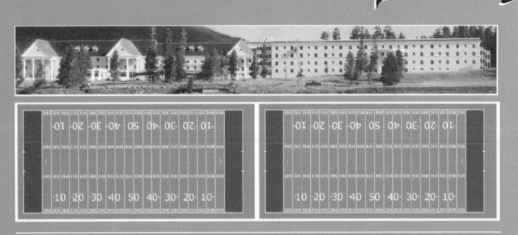

The Lake Hotel sprawls 720 feet in length, which equals the size of two side-by-side football fields. Guests who stay in the far end of the east wing must literally walk the length of two football fields to reach the dining room, on the hotel's west end. *[Photo courtesy of the author]*

- **Original Color:** Debatable. Today's painters see evidence of an original white coat of paint. But they say that the white may have been a primer, not the actual color. Historical records show the hotel has definitely been yellow since the late 1890s.

- **Why Yellow:** Railroad hotels often were painted yellow, and the Northern Pacific Railroad bankrolled the Lake Hotel's 1890 construction. Architect Robert Reamer likely stayed with the color because in the early 1900s, medium-yellow—called "Colonial Yellow"—was a popular choice for exterior walls of Colonial Revival style buildings. Henry Flagler painted his Florida chain of resort hotels Colonial Yellow with white trim; the Yellowstone Park Association may have copied, wanting to provide familiarity to East Coast guests.[3]

A Fine Place to Dine

In 1912, Robert Reamer had expanded the dining room, adding a polygon-shaped addition at the west end of the hotel. Reamer also created free-standing, ivory-enameled, Ionic-column lamps that mirrored the hotel's exterior columns. Each lamp was topped by an enameled wood bowl that held four fifty-watt light bulbs, providing a soft glow for surrounding diners.[4]

By 1923, though, especially with the addition of the 113-room east wing, the dining room once again needed to grow. This time, Link & Haire handled the project. The architects tore down the 1912 addition and then doubled the dining room's size, once again adding the polygonal design on the west end. When finished, the dining room could seat four hundred guests and offered lovely lake views.

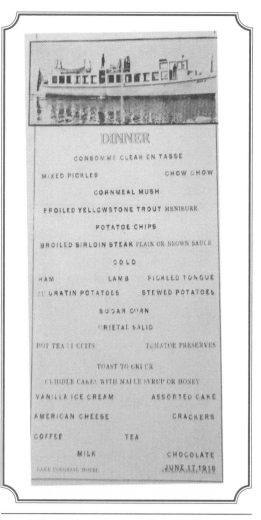

Above: This Lake Hotel menu shows the type of food that guests dined on in 1916. [*Photo courtesy of the National Park Service, Yellowstone National Park Research Center*]

Left: The newly renovated dining room featured birch chairs with cane seats; freshly picked wildflowers on the tables; and an all-female waitstaff, reminiscent of the famous Harvey Girls. [*Photo courtesy of the Montana Historical Society Research Center*]

Right: The Batchelder tile fireplace attracts the eyes of guests, many who want to know its history. [*Photo courtesy of Xanterra Parks & Resorts*]

Below: The Batchelder drinking fountain still works, providing a pleasant scene for the thirsty. [*Photo courtesy of the author*]

Batchelder Fireplace and Fountain

Guests often touch—even stroke—the tiles of the lobby's massive Arts and Crafts fireplace. Some mistake the tile as Rookwood Pottery of Cincinnati, Ohio, but in truth, Robert Reamer turned to Ernest Batchelder of Pasadena, California, in 1923 to create this one-of-a-kind fireplace.

Seventeen feet, ten inches wide by seven feet, ten inches tall, the fireplace features two large, forest-themed tiles and thirteen pine cone motif tiles. A matching water fountain, located to the right of the fireplace, was installed in 1926 and commands equal admiration.[5]

Savages!

At one time, everybody had a nickname in Yellowstone, and some nicknames endure, like "savages," which refers to park employees.

Most names have faded in popularity. Guests, for instance, were once known as "dudes" or "sagebrushers." A dude arrived by train, traveled by stagecoach or touring car, and lodged in hotels. A sagebrusher toured the park on their own, and camped.

Other nicknames:

- **Dishwashers:** pearl divers
- **Waitresses:** heavers
- **Housekeepers:** pillow punchers
- **Bus drivers:** gear jammers (or jammers)
- **Laundry women:** bubble queens
- **Porters / bell boys:** pack rats (or rats)[6]

Above: In the 1950s and 1960s, many employees had personalized, keepsake mugs made at a curio shop in West Yellowstone. *[Photo courtesy of Joshua D. Stein]*
Opposite: This 1928 photo, shot in front of the dining room, shows heavers, pillow punchers, and pack rats. The two nurses in front would have worked in the on-site dispensary, which was then located in the hallway, across from today's deli. *[Photo courtesy of the Montana Historical Society Research Center]*

Presidential Suite

When Link & Haire expanded the dining room in 1923, they also added a second floor above it, to house a series of rooms—including the Presidential Suite. The addition featured seven connecting bedrooms and four bathrooms that could be configured in various ways, depending on the size of the party. President Calvin Coolidge stayed here in 1927; up until the 1980s, a plaque outside the suite memorialized this fact. More often, the suite hosted Park President Harry Child and his wife, Adelaide.

There's a story told about Child and how he enjoyed touring the park in his Lincoln Phaeton, followed by a yellow touring car holding his grandchildren, nieces, and nephews. When they arrived at the Lake Hotel, however, Child and his wife retired to the Presidential Suite and the children were banished to the east wing—on the opposite end.

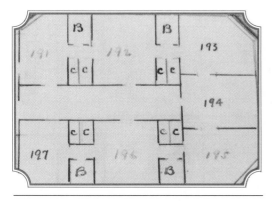

This hand-drawn schematic shows the original layout of the Presidential Suite. [*Photo courtesy of the National Park Service, Yellowstone National Park Research Center*]

Presidential Visitors

Several U.S. Presidents have visited the Lake Hotel (or tried to visit), but just one sitting president—Calvin Coolidge—has spent the night.

1903: President Theodore Roosevelt spent two weeks vacationing in Yellowstone; during his visit, he laid the cornerstone for the Roosevelt Arch in Gardiner, Montana. He wanted to stay at the Lake Hotel, but it was April, and the hotel was closed. Surprisingly, the winter keeper—whose politics, perhaps, differed from Roosevelt's—refused to open up the hotel for the president, saying it was too much work!

[Photos courtesy of the National Park Service]

1923: In July, President Warren Harding toured the park, fed bears, and visited the lake area—some of the last recreations he would enjoy. One month later, he unexpectedly died in San Francisco of possible heart failure.

1927: President Calvin Coolidge (front right) and his family toured the park and stayed in the Lake Hotel's Presidential Suite. During the visit, Park Superintendent Horace Albright (front left) tried to talk politics, but "Silent Cal" sidestepped such conversation. Albright wanted the Grand Tetons—not yet a national park—to be folded into Yellowstone, but the President was more interested in scoring an extra night at the hotel, so he could check out a new fishing hole!

1993: President Jimmy Carter vacationed in Yellowstone during his presidency, but the trip did not include an overnight stay at the Lake Hotel. In 1993, Jimmy and Rosalynn stayed at the Lake Hotel, at least two nights, but not in the Presidential Suite (it was already reserved, so they chose a lake view room).[7] The Carters ate in the dining room, and also feasted on pizza in the lake area's employee pub, where the President signed his name—in pink ink—on the pub wall (an employee tradition).

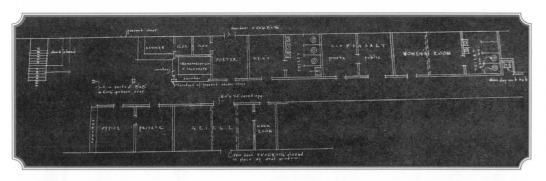

1924: Hallway Makeover

Between 1904 and 1924, mostly guest rooms and communal baths occupied the hotel's main-floor hallway (which today connects the registration desk with the east wing lobby). But in 1923, with the east wing completed, guests now had to walk through this bedroom-heavy hallway to reach the main lobby and dining room.

The time had come for change.

Architects Link & Haire handled this project, gutting fifteen guest rooms and installing a hallway bursting with guest-friendly services: a two-room dispensary staffed by on-duty nurses and doctors; transportation and telegraph counters; and a Grille, which likely served up burgers and other casual food. Most noteworthy: the Haynes Picture Store, one of many that served guests in the park.

1928: Refreshment Parlor

In 1928, park leaders brought architect Robert Reamer back to the Lake Hotel to begin his final projects—his finishing touches. This time, Reamer focused on expanding the lobby, creating an intimate north wing near the Batchelder fireplace and a cavernous horseshoe-shaped south wing, that would hold the sunroom.

Above, left: This Link & Haire blueprint shows what the hotel's main-floor hallway looked like after the 1924 renovation. The Grille was located where today's deli sits, and it provided entrances from both inside and outside of the hotel. A card room replaced the Grille in 1929. [*Photo courtesy of the National Park Service, Yellowstone National Park Archives*]

The Coat Controversy of 1924

By 1924, not everyone who came to the Lake Hotel stayed overnight. Much like today, some just popped in for a look-see, and maybe a meal. But in those years, the Lake Hotel (like every Yellowstone hotel) required men to wear a jacket in the dining room. It didn't matter if the guest was camping nearby, just passing through, or if their jacket was buried deep inside of their luggage.

Jackets were required.

Somehow, though, the jacket issue snagged the attention of Stephen Mather, head of the National Park Service. Mather, a self-made millionaire, sided with Yellowstone guests, ruling that men on vacation should not be required to wear a formal jacket while dining. But Yellowstone park leaders—many of whom well remembered the hotel's early, genteel etiquette—side-stepped the ruling, stocking their own jackets that men could "borrow" while dining in their establishments.[8]

[*Photo courtesy of antiqueimages.blog.com*]

The Haynes Picture Store nestled into the corner now occupied by the porter's desk. What's most interesting about this photo is the plain door on the left; today, guests enter or exit the hotel to the back parking lot at this same location, but through wide double doors. [*Photo courtesy of the Montana Historical Society Research Center*]

The Haynes Picture Store pictured here in the new refreshment parlor, did good business in the 1920s at the Lake Hotel. Frank Jay Haynes, Yellowstone's most prolific photographer, started shooting images of the park in the 1880s. After he retired in 1916, his son, Jack—also a talented photographer—took over and managed the Haynes stores park-wide until his death in the 1960s. At the Lake Hotel, Jack Ellis Haynes operated a darkroom in a cubby space tucked beneath the ground floor stairs, near today's deli. [*Photo courtesy of the Montana Historical Society Research Center*]

The north wing now houses the hotel's gift shop; but in 1928, Reamer's blueprint shows it held a buffet, a curio counter, and the Haynes Picture Store. Guests could also lounge at tables in the room's center, known as the refreshment parlor.

After Prohibition ended in 1933, this space evolved into two bars—the first named the Rainbow Lounge, followed by the Dry Dock Lounge in the 1970s.

1929 Census Reveals Much About the Lake Hotel

In 1929, park leaders commissioned an inventory census of the Lake Hotel that today reveals much about the hotel's early days.

For instance, the hotel once had what's called an annunciator system, a communications device that connected guest rooms to the porter desk. Whether the guest needed a bucket of ice or help down with their luggage, they simply pushed a button in their room, triggering the annunciator board. A bell rang and an arrow wiggled over the room number; then a bellboy trotted to the room to help.

The annunciator system vanished from the Lake Hotel long ago, but the arrow-wiggling annunciator board lives on behind today's porter desk.

A blueprint of Robert Reamer's north wing refreshment parlor, built in 1928. [*Photo courtesy of the National Park Service, Yellowstone National Park Archives*]

Jack Ellis Haynes operated a darkroom in a cubby space tucked beneath the ground floor stairs, near today's deli.

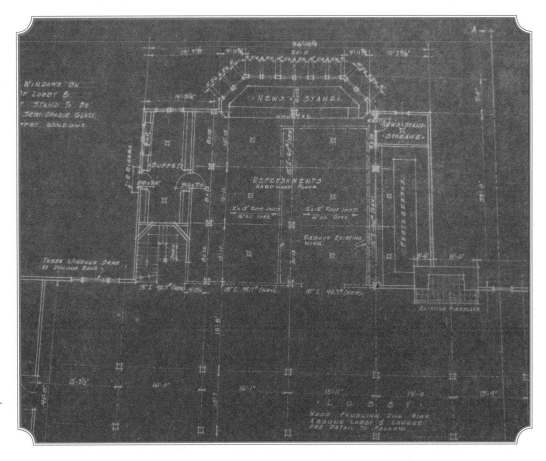

Beyond the annunciator system, the census methodically listed everything of worth in the hotel. Here are a few inventory items, with photos that give an idea of what those items looked like.

1. Shoe Shine Parlor

Gentlemen in 1929 ventured into the hotel's basement for a shoe shine (that staircase is located left of the gift shop). Much like the shoe shine stand pictured here, the hotel's shoe shine business featured two leather seats, a paneled (wood) back and ends, and a two-step base, with linoleum beneath its iron footrests. The shoe shine parlor's value: $85 ($1,174 today).[9]

[Photo courtesy of liveauctioneers.com]

2. Blue Willow Ware

In the summer of 2013, this author spied half of a blue-and-white coffee cup, unearthed by workmen, behind the hotel. It turned out to be blue willow ware, the Lake Hotel's predominate dish style, according to the 1929 census. The cup was likely Buffalo Pottery's blue willow ware (made in Buffalo, New York), a style and product utilized heavily by restaurants nationwide. The hotel's coffee cup inventory in 1929 was valued at $143.10 (or $1,962 in modern terms).[10]

For the record, the coffee cup was sent to Yellowstone's Heritage and Research Center in Gardiner, Montana.

[Photo courtesy of the author]

3. Wireless #12 Cigar Lighter

The hotel's curio counter (today's gift shop) offered one of these lighters for guest use. Made by Eldred Manufacturing Company in Chicago, Illinois, the lighter was valued at $17.50 ($242 today).[11] Smokers simply pulled the brass arm forward to produce a spark, which then ignited a fuel-soaked wick.

[Photo courtesy of iCollector.com]

4. Cig-ash-adors

Smokers ruled in the 1920s, and ashtrays abounded throughout the hotel. Cigar smokers in 1929 could puff away freely in the Lake Hotel's card room (today's deli), with all brass Cig-ash-adors provided to collect the big butts (valued at $21 then—$290 in modern dollars).[12]

[Photo courtesy of iCollector.com]

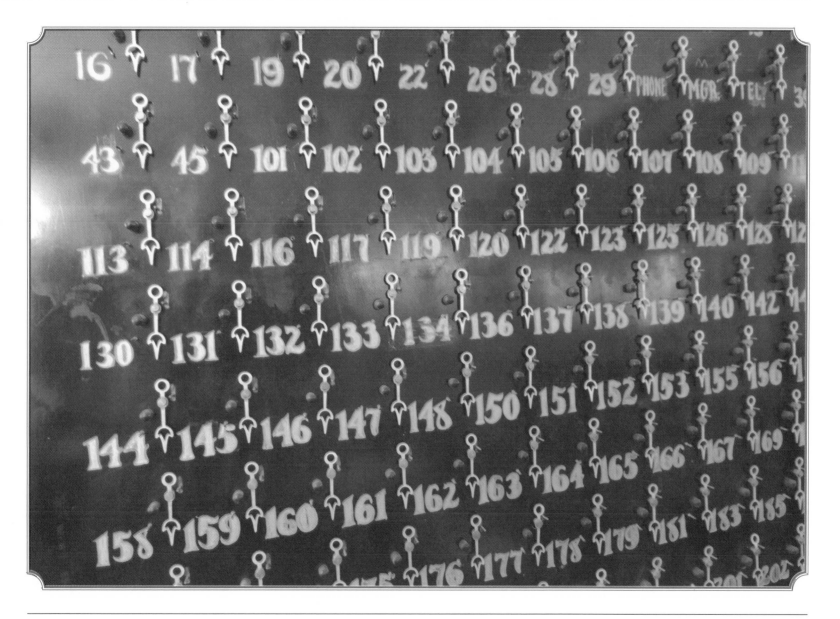

The Lake Hotel's annunciator board. [*Photo courtesy of the author*]

Colonial to Queen Anne

Robert Reamer certainly was not shy about switching up the Lake Hotel, even if it meant colliding styles. This becomes obvious when climbing the central grand staircase, which starts in the lobby, next to the concierge desk.

In 1928, Reamer installed a Colonial Revival staircase, with its distinctive curl-out banister, but only between the ground and first floors. He kept the original, 1891 Queen Anne–style staircase intact between the first and second floors. In doing so, Reamer literally connected the hotel's 1891 beginning with its 1929 completion.

Above: The hotel's original 1891 Queen Anne-style staircase merges with a Colonial Revival staircase installed by Robert Reamer in 1928. *[Photo courtesy of the author]*

Left: Robert Reamer's blueprint details the hotel's Colonial Revival staircase. *[Photo courtesy of the National Park Service, Yellowstone National Park Archives]*

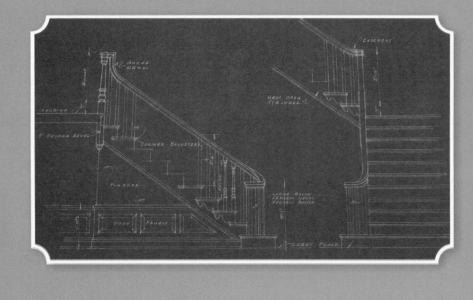

Crowning Touch: The Reamer Lounge

Twenty-five years after he began his transformation of the Lake Hotel, Robert Reamer created his final, crowning touch—this time, going out of his way to show off the lake area's natural beauty. He designed a horseshoe-shaped sunroom that juts south from the hotel's lobby, giving it a special, almost stand-alone feel. Then he lined the room with large windows, providing guests with a 180-degree view of Yellowstone Lake and the surrounding mountains.

Before construction could begin, however, workmen had to move the original *porte cochére* from the hotel's center columns to its present location—between the center and east-end columns. In 1938, the *porte cochére* would be expanded from three to six bays.

With the *porte cochére* out of the way, Reamer built the sunroom, which was known then as the Reamer Lounge. In those days (as is true now), it became the place where guests gravitated in the morning for coffee and reading, in the

This 1929 photo of the Reamer Lounge was shot from the far end of the room, looking back toward the refreshment parlor, where today's gift shop is located. If the hotel has a heart, it is here, in this room with a view. [*Photo courtesy of the Montana Historical Society Research Center*]

afternoon for postcards and conversation, and in the evening for music and libations.

The sunroom's completion was indeed a crowning moment and should have meant that the Lake Hotel's best days were ahead. But fate had others plans for the Grand Lady of the Lake.

∿ 6 ∿
THE DARK YEARS (1930–1945)

The celebration of the Lake Hotel's completion was extremely short lived. When America's stock market crashed in October of 1929, the Lake Hotel's fortunes crashed right along with it. Suddenly, the grand hotel lost its luster, its appeal. Yellowstone, once a playground for the wealthy, was now a destination for the masses that preferred simple, affordable cabins over big, fancy hotels.

It was a moment of reckoning for park leaders. The Lake Hotel had been built for train-traveling, stagecoach-riding guests of means. Now economics presented a new breed of traveler: independent and anxious to save a buck.

Unsure of what to do, park leaders considered turning the hotel into a resort, a place where guests came for a week or two (or maybe the entire summer) to ride horses, go fishing, and enjoy live entertainment.

To gauge interest, management mailed a letter and brochure detailing the resort to one hundred former guests. They also contacted Irving "Larry" Larom, owner of The Valley Ranch in Valley, Wyoming, and founding president of the Dude Ranchers' Association. If the plan flew, Larom would outfit their multiday pack rides.

"A most popular [pack trip] would, of course, be down along the east shore of the Lake, into the southeast arms of Bridger Lake and [the] Thorofare sections,"[1] Larom wrote Park President William Nichols in

December 1931 (longtime park president Harry Child died that same year). The Thorofare, on Yellowstone Lake's south end, represents the park's most remote acreage.

Costs varied, but a room with a bath, all meals, a boat rental, and the use of a horse ran a party of two $145 a week—or $2,229 today (the dollar was not worth as much during the Depression).[2]

Opposite: The clouds hovering over the Lake Hotel in this 1937 image look as ominous as the closed hotel's uncertain status in the 1930s and 1940s. *[Photo courtesy of the National Park Service, Yellowstone National Park YELL#122361]* Above: Park leaders considered adding pack trips as a Lake Hotel activity. *[Photo courtesy of the National Park Service]*

> **❝** I understand there has developed a new type of tourist who prefer[s] cabins with hotel comforts, and [is] willing to pay approximately hotel rates. **❞**

Alas, the big plan—a full year in the making—petered out in the spring of 1932, when only two former guests responded to the query letter, and neither planned to visit Yellowstone anytime soon.[3] The Lake Hotel limped through just one month that summer and—with official permission from the U.S. Department of the Interior—closed without ceremony on July 15.[4]

Five long years would pass before the Grand Lady greeted another guest.

The Lake Hotel's Great Depression
Park leaders had plenty of time to consider the future of their now dormant Lake Hotel. But the thought of tearing down one of the park's earliest inns—or altering Robert Reamer's work in any way—pained them.

Oddly enough, when leaders asked Reamer what to do, the architect offered this insight: "All over the country, cabins are becoming more in demand," he wrote Park President William Nichols in 1934. "As a matter of fact, I understand there has developed a new type of tourist who prefer[s] cabins with hotel comforts, and

[is] willing to pay approximately hotel rates."[5]

In 1935, Reamer sent Nichols blueprints detailing how the hotel he'd spent twenty-five years molding might be carved up to make it more guest-friendly. The architect proposed splitting the hotel in half and obliterating the center section. In addition, Reamer recommended slicing off the second and third floors of the Old House (the original hotel), which would have meant the removal of the exterior Colonial Revival columns. The benefit of such a major change: guests could pull up between the two remaining sections of the hotel, check in, and continue driving straight back to the yet-to-be-built cottages. Only the hotel's east-wing rooms would have survived.

But Nichols remained in wait-and-see mode. And in 1936, with park attendance on the rise, he must have felt optimistic, because he approved a roof job for the still-closed hotel.

When the hotel finally reopened in the summer of 1937, everything from a guest's perspective appeared to be back to normal. But attendance still lagged, causing park leaders to mull new

options. Decisions toughened in 1938 when Robert Reamer died, leaving the park without its longtime architectural leader.

Fortunately, change often comes slowly in Yellowstone. For the moment, the Lake Hotel remained intact.

The Calm Before the Storm
After the thrifty Great Depression, train travelers still took the Grand Tour, circling the park by bus and spending at least one night at the Lake Hotel. Automobile tourists, though, drove here, there, and everywhere. And they typically camped or stayed in low-cost cabins.

So the Lake Hotel sat, half empty, lacking the pow of an Old Faithful geyser or the wow of the Grand Canyon of the Yellowstone. When it reopened in 1937, the hotel earned a mere $33,559 from lodging, compared to the $91,153 raked in by the Old Faithful Inn.[6]

Park leaders continued to agonize over what to do. And in 1939, sentiment must have turned toward saving the hotel, because a query went out to Stroheim & Romann in New York, seeking

The Lake Hotel appears to be business as usual in 1937, with guests enjoying an evening in the Reamer Lounge. *[Photo courtesy of the Montana Historical Society Research Center]*

Reamer's Two-Fold Proposal

Robert Reamer proposed major changes to the Lake Hotel in 1935, which he detailed on two blueprints. This first blueprint of the hotel's Old House shows that the lobby staircase is gone—because the second and third floors have been removed. The estimated cost for this renovation, written on the blueprint, was $5,000—nearly $86,000 in today's dollars.[7] In a letter to Park President William Nichols, Reamer explained the first blueprint:

66 *Sheet #1 is a plan for the present lobby and dining room end of the hotel. At the rear, and behind the fireplace, an entrance is provided [that] leads directly into the lunch room, barber shop, beauty parlor, and toilets. Such an entrance seems necessary and would naturally be used by the cottage guests. I have partially screened this entrance off from the main lounge, partly for privacy and partly to give a better sitting space around the fireplace. The main dining room has been reduced about twenty feet in length to permit [for] the cocktail room. You will notice I have given up the stairs to the basement, which, as I remember, did not amount to much; and, of course, you gain the room now occupied by the main stairs up. The lounge or dance floor would be the same size as at present except for about ten feet devoted to the cocktail room.[8]* 99

1.

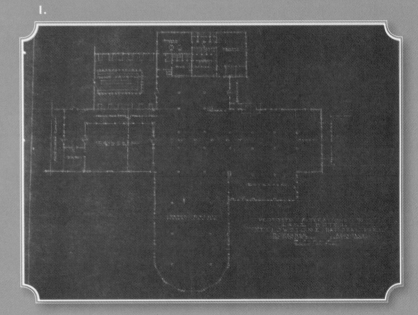

2.

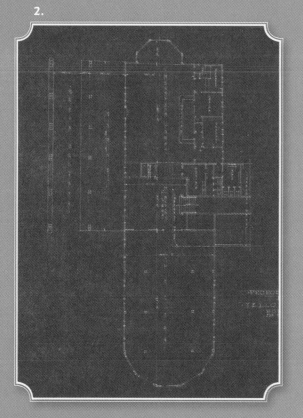

This second blueprint shows how Reamer would have altered the current east-wing lobby to include the registration desk, lounge, and *porte cochére*. It seems askew, because the *porte cochére*—which now faces east–west—is repositioned to face north–south. The new alignment would have allowed guests to pull up between the two sections of the remaining hotel to register and then continue on to the cabins (or park and settle into an east-wing room). The cost estimate written on the blueprint: $16,000 (close to $275,000 today).[9] Here's how Reamer explained this scenario:

> 66 *Sheet #2 shows suggested alterations to the room end of [the] hotel, which includes a business lobby with the needed facilities, the porte cochére, and a lounge for the hotel guests. The location of the elevator is not changed; that is, if the elevator is where I have reason to believe it is. You may think the lounge in this building is too large or unnecessary. By knocking out some of the rooms on the ground floor, you might get a lounge that would answer the purpose at a considerable saving[s] but, of course, would not be as spectacular. It all depends on what result you wish to obtain.* [10] 99

Opposite and left: *[Photo courtesy of National Park Service, Yellowstone National Park Archives]*

> **" In a spirit of joie de vivre, we gaily tore down the wing we built in 1903, thereby destroying some fifty or sixty perfectly good rooms. "**

the availability of yellow-and-turquoise novelty cloth (presumably to reupholster the wicker furniture).[11] Similarly, a letter was mailed to Hazel Wray Davey in Los Angeles, requesting additional hotel curtains.

Both requests were soon rescinded, however. "Since writing you, our plans have changed," President Nichols curtly wrote Davey in July of that same year.[12] And with that letter, a new, not so favorable course of action was set in motion.

The End of the Ell

After a decade of hand wringing over what to do about the Lake Hotel, park leaders finally caved in to public demand and decided to build

cottages behind the hotel in 1940. They also decided to tear down the ell (the north-jutting wing that Robert Reamer built in 1903). The rest of the hotel also appeared to be on the chopping block—so much so that a Livingston apartment complex wrote park leaders, wanting the building's elevator. (Park President Nichols wrote back, saying the park had its own plan for the elevator).[13]

"Before the war, we persuaded ourselves that what we wanted at the Lake was a comparatively modest hotel and cottages, the same as we have at Mammoth now," Nichols wrote in 1951. "And in a spirit of joie de vivre, we gaily tore down the wing we built in 1903, thereby destroying some

This aerial view of the hotel and cabins, which likely dates from the late 1950s or early 1960s, clearly shows the location of the original cabins—built on the hotel property's west end (where today's post office is located). *[Photo courtesy of the National Park Service, Yellowstone National Park YELL#143033-b]*

Left: Rear Admiral Luther Sheldon, Jr. *[Photo courtesy of the National Library of Medicine]*

Far Left: The Ahwahnee hotel in Yosemite was temporarily transformed into a U.S. naval hospital, known as Yosemite Special Hospital, on June 25, 1943. The thirty-seven-acre complex, renovated for recuperating sailors, included a library, six-lane bowling alley, and pool hall.[18] *[Photo courtesy of the National Park Service]*

fifty or sixty perfectly good rooms...but...Gee!... It made a grand parking space in back of the hotel!"[14]

After the ell came down, park leaders closed the hotel, and nobody knew if or when it would reopen. Indeed, in January of 1940, Park Attorney Hugh Galusha wrote the Internal Revenue Service, stating that "the Yellowstone Park Company plan[s], now, on demolishing the Lake Hotel," and asking about the rate of depreciation if the process were spread over three years. "One reason that this would extend over a period of three years is that more or less of the material would be used in the construction of cabins, and they would take the material from the building as they would need it," he wrote.[15]

True to this line of thinking, cottage construction began in 1941, using wood and windows

salvaged from the ell's demolition.

It sounds strange to say that anything about World War II was fortuitous, but in 1942, the war stopped all park construction projects—and possible demolitions. For the war's duration, the cabins remained unfinished, and the Lake Hotel sat nearly empty; most furniture and rugs went into storage, or was sent to other park hotels. For the moment, the Grand Lady dodged the wrecking ball.

The War Years

Yellowstone remained open during World War II—but barely. Gas rationing and other wartime restrictions sharply curtailed American vacations. Those who did venture to Yellowstone in 1943 discovered closed park hotels, lodges, and cafeterias. A coffee shop in Mammoth Hot Springs served food; and the park-wide Hamilton stores

offered gasoline, food, and limited lodging. Mostly, though, the war years decimated park attendance figures, which plummeted from 567,437 in 1940 to a scant 64,144 in 1943.[16]

Unexpectedly, 1943 offered the Lake Hotel a shot at a new life. Rear Admiral Luther Sheldon, Jr., the U.S. Navy's assistant chief in the Bureau of Medicine and Surgery, toured Yellowstone hotels to see if any were "satisfactory for conversion into convalescent hospitals."[17] Yosemite National Park's hotel, The Ahwahnee, had recently been converted for such use. In the end, Yellowstone's harsh winter temperatures likely dissuaded the military from sending soldiers there to recuperate.

And so, the Lake Hotel—shut down and facing possible demolition—lost a key opportunity to not just be useful again, but to be a healing place for the war's wounded.

Iconic Yellow Bus Rolls for Decades

When the stagecoach left the park in 1917, replaced by the automobile, the park needed another way to shuttle guests. A bright-yellow touring vehicle, built by the White Motor Company of Cleveland, Ohio, proved to be the best choice.

The earliest vehicles were convertibles, followed by crank-engine buses with roofs and open-air windows. Finally, between 1936 and 1939, the park invested in ninety-eight buses that featured roll-back canvas roofs, enabling guests to stand and view animals from the safety of the vehicle.

The thirteen-passenger buses roamed Yellowstone for the next three decades, carrying guests to geysers, animals, and sunsets. Drivers were nicknamed "gear jammers," because they often had to ram the tough double clutches into gear. During World War II, though, the park saw far fewer guests, and the buses did not roll as much.

After the war, park attendance skyrocketed, but two national phenomena greatly affected bus patronage: President Dwight D. Eisenhower massively expanded the country's highway system, and more Americans could afford automobiles. Sadly, by the late 1960s, the historic yellow buses had—like the Lake Hotel— become a relic of the past. Even sadder, park officials sold all but one bus, mostly to private investors across the United States (two other buses would eventually be added to the park's vehicle collection).

Just like the stagecoach before it, the yellow bus disappeared, seemingly forever.

Stretching twenty-five feet in length, White Motor Company's Model 706 featured lantern-style rear lights, a six-cylinder engine, and a roll-back canvas roof. *[Photo courtesy of Joshua D. Stein]*

ellowstone was ill-prepared for the end of World War II. In the summer of 1945, tourists flooded the park in such droves that park officials issued a "special announcement" stressing the importance of advance reservations.

"Due to [the] lifting of gas rationing and release of war workers, travel to Yellowstone Park is three times as heavy as this time last year. Eating and housing facilities are limited and those coming to the Park should have confirmed reservations for rooms, or come prepared to take care of themselves in the public camp grounds."[1]

After five years of sitting empty and idle, the Lake Hotel was in no shape to house the deluge of visitors, which totaled 178,296 in summer 1945. Nor was the Grand Dame ready to accommodate guests in 1946, when park attendance ballooned to 814,907.[2] Yellowstone's other hotels and lodges also needed repairs, and the nearly-demolished Lake Hotel was low on the list for the limited supply of carpenters, painters, and skilled laborers.

Finally, in 1947, desperate to provide additional lodging, park leaders patched up the Lake Hotel's more modern east wing and opened it to guests. The following year, a decision was made to put the once grand hotel "back in A-1 shape."[3]

The Lake Hotel was on the unexpected road to recovery.

The Lady Finally Gets a Makeover

After World War II ended, the Lake Hotel—now more than fifty years old—was well past her prime, but the immense building contained more than one hundred and seventy much-needed rooms.

So in 1950, park leaders invested heavily in her recovery, spending nearly $75,000 ($735,000 in today's dollars) plastering and repainting fifty-five rooms, and the hotel hallways. The next year, an additional $23,477 ($230,000 today) paid for the repair of eighty rooms; and in 1952, $23,285 was spent updating thirty-seven rooms.[4]

Opposite: By 1950, the entire Lake Hotel was up and running once again. Note the wide web-threaded chairs, different from the wicker furniture that architect Robert Reamer introduced in the 1920s. *[Photo courtesy of the Montana Historical Society Research Center]*

Above: The Lake Hotel again served guests in the late 1940s, but the lodging is not mentioned in this 1949 park brochure. *[Photo courtesy of the author]*

Right: In 1950, the hotel's curio shop and newsstand reopened after a ten-year hiatus. It sprawled across the back wall of what today is the hotel's gift shop. *[Photo courtesy of the Montana Historical Society Research Center]*

More than $40,000 ($392,000 today) was then laid out on furnishings and everything else needed to outfit the hotel, as well as the forty-three just-finished cabins located behind the hotel. Items purchased ranged from beds and mattresses to dressers and night tables, as well as toilets, ashtrays and a Hoover vacuum cleaner.[5]

In 1950, the Lake Hotel brought in nearly $82,000 in lodging profits, huge for a hotel that had been slated for demolition, but a pittance compared to the nearly $147,000 that the Canyon Hotel earned.[6] Still, all things considered, the Grand Lady of the Lake was definitely on the mend.

In 1951, park leaders turned to a Los Angeles company named Calif-Asia Rattan Company to obtain the peel-cane winding material needed to repair the hotel's aging lounge chairs. Long, cushioned couches also appeared for the first time in the Reamer Lounge, now called the sunroom. *[Photo courtesy of the Montana Historical Society Research Center]*

Dining Room Reopens— as a Coffee Shop

After two years of renovations, the once-elegant Lake Hotel dining room reopened—as a more humble coffee shop. Throngs of bus tourists, who in previous years had stopped at the nearby Lake Lodge for lunch, now descended on the hotel, to eat such fare as baked filet of whitefish *à la créole*, Irish lamb stew, and baked macaroni and ham.

Beyond the coffee shop's opening, the year 1953 also marked when the Lake Hotel once again earned mention in park guides and brochures. Such publications stopped featuring the hotel as a possible lodging stop in 1940.

Room prices varied, but the hotel's American Plan, which included lodging and three meals per day, cost $10.50 per person without a bathroom and $13 a night with a bathroom ($93 and $115 respectively in today's dollars).[7] Amenities included steam heat and hot and cold running water, as well as barber, telegraph, and laundry services.[8]

Simple Cottages Built as a Hotel Alternative

As early as 1934, architect Robert Reamer pitched the idea of building cottages behind the hotel.

"My idea is that the group of cabins should have the appearance of a village rather than a row of miners' cabins," Reamer wrote Park President William Nichols, referring to cabin projects at the Mammoth Hot Springs Hotel and the Lake Hotel. "They should be different as to the exterior and painted or stained in different, harmonious colors."[9]

The Lake Hotel's current cabin complex does resemble a village of sorts, but all of the simple, prefabricated cottages, single or double, look almost identical. They're all painted yellow—though early color suggestions included gray and brown.

Construction started in 1941, but shut down during World War II. Twenty-two single cabins and twenty-one double cabins sat unfinished until 1950, when money and manpower finally allowed completion.

After a 13-year hiatus, the Lake Hotel dining room reopened in 1953, but as a coffee shop. *[Photo courtesy of the Montana Historical Society Research Center]*

The original cottages opened to guests in the 1950s. They continue to be the hotel's most rustic lodging option. *[Photo courtesy of the Montana Historical Society Research Center]*

This picture of the Island Fish Fry illustrates what the site looked like in the 1930s. *[Photo courtesy of the National Park Service, Yellowstone National Park YELL#89236]*

"The first one was occupied on July 15, 1950," Nichols wrote in 1951. "In fact, I have the first dollar we ever got from the investment in cottages. It is framed and in my office."[10]

By 1953, fifty more cottages had been built. Unlike the original cottages, which strung along the parking lot where today's post office sits, the new cabins sprang up north of what is now the Sandpiper Lodge. In the late 1950s, the original cottages were moved to the current cabin complex, bringing the total number of cabins to 110.

Today the cabins are the Lake Hotel's most affordable lodging option, each outfitted with two double beds and a bathroom. Guests enjoy all hotel amenities, including the business center, dining room, and nightly music in the sunroom.

Island Fish Fry Held on Stevenson Island

Between 1936 and 1941, park guests could spend the day fishing on Yellowstone Lake and eating what they caught at an afternoon fish fry held on Stevenson Island (the island directly in front of the Lake Hotel).

World War II put an end to the popular activity, but in 1959, park leaders decided to give the fish fry another go.

This 1950s-era advertisement promoted the Island Fish Fry, which offered guests an afternoon of fishing on the lake followed by a freshly-cooked meal on Stevenson Island. *[Photo courtesy of the National Park Service, Yellowstone National Park YELL#193429]*

In 1963, Lloyd Wood worked as a cook's helper at the Lake Lodge, and one day a week he served as the fill-in cook at the Island Fish Fry. Here's how Wood, now living in Amarillo, Texas, explains the event:

"I would be taken from the hotel marina to the island by a [fishing] guide. I had a helper with me who washed dishes and helped with the service. We would get to the island dock around 9 AM. [Then] I would get some lake water in a large coffee pot and make the old-style 'cowboy coffee' [coffee made without a filter] on a stove in the cook shack. After I got the coffee brewing, I [took] my fishing rod and fish[ed] off of the dock, until the guests started arriving. The guides would take their customers out on the lake to fish. When [each guest] had their limit, which I believe was three fish or ten pounds, whichever came first, they [came] to the island. There, the guides would clean and filet the fish; and we would fry them and serve them, with French fries and a salad. I think they had a choice of coffee or iced tea. After they were finished, they [were] taken back to the hotel. Our day would end about 5 PM, after we had cleaned up." [11]

The Island Fish Fry ran from late June to early September and typically attracted around twelve hundred guests. It ended in the mid-1960s, after the marina was moved from the Lake Hotel to Bridge Bay, and has yet to return.

7 LAKE AREA
Stevenson Island Fish Fry is a Park "must."

Picturesque Lake Hotel on the shore of Yellowstone Lake . . . "mother" to fishermen, native cutthroat trout, and boats of varying sizes.

The Deadly Quake of '59

At 11:37 PM on August 17, 1959, a 7.5 magnitude earthquake severely shook the earth at Hebgen Lake, about twenty miles northwest of West Yellowstone. Twenty-eight people, mostly campers, died after a mountainside sheared off and buried everything below.

Nearly ninety miles southeast of the quake epicenter, many Lake Hotel guests were jolted awake in their beds. Many jumped up, packed their bags, and checked out immediately—only to discover buckled, impassable park roads.

Beyond scaring the wits out of guests, the quake caused little damage to the hotel. Take a close look at the fireplace mantel today: the quake dislodged it from the wall. It was long ago repaired, but still appears slightly wavy—a reminder of that wobbly night at the Lake Hotel.

The earthquake was reported far and wide, including in the *Newburgh-Beacon News* in Newburgh, New York, which carried this headline and an Associated Press story on September 1, 1959. *[Photo courtesy of the Newburgh-Beacon News]*

TUESDAY, SEPTEMBER 1, 1959

Quake Death Toll Now Listed at 28

WEST YELLOWSTONE, Mont. (AP) — "The evidence available indicates they probably were in the slide area."

With those words Monday, Sheriff Donald J. Skerritt added 13 names, raising to 28 the probable death toll in the mammoth landslides set off by earthquakes Aug. 17-18.

"We've checked and checked every lead on all these people," the sheriff said. "We've found no trace of any of them since."

Among the 13 were Robert J. Williams, 32, his wife and three children, Michael, 7, Christy, 3, and Steven, 11, of Idaho Falls, Idaho.

Williams was due back to work Monday as manager of the plumbing and building department of an Idaho Falls store. He did not report. Twenty-four hours before the quake he registered at Virginia City Museum near the center of the disaster.

Also on the list are Roger Provost, associate warden at Soledad, Calif., medium security prison, his wife and two sons.

His mother, Katherine Provost, Ontario, Calif., received the last word on a post card mailed Aug. 16 at West Yellowstone.

"We are camped on Madison River 30 miles from Yellowstone," Provost wrote. "It's a beautiful place. Fishing fair."

Millions of tons of rock and earth crashed down on that area, damming the river and forming a new lake.

The 13 include Dr. Merle Edgerton and wife, Edna, and Harmon Woods and wife, all of Coalinga, Calif., who were traveling together. Dr. Edgerton failed to return for appointments with patients a week after the quakes. Relatives consider all four dead.

A young Dick Crysdale, who worked as a fishing guide, was attending a dance held in the Lake Hotel sunroom when the quake hit. Crysdale writes about his experience in his book, *Yellowstone, Cutthroats, and Me: A Fishing Guide's Autobiography*:

Fishing guide, Dick Crysdale, assisted Lake Hotel guests who refused to return to their rooms after the late-night earthquake. *[Photo courtesy of Dick Crysdale]*

66 *The live band was in the area of the bay windows which overlooked Yellowstone Lake. Ellen Lichtenstein was rocking and rolling with me. Suddenly, the wooden floor began to undulate like gentle waves washing up on a beach. Ellen and I were almost knocked over. The windows began to rattle. The lobby pillars were swaying. A low, ominous rumble accompanied the movement, and the whole lobby squeaked.*

We stopped dancing and I looked around to find what might be causing this weird experience. The pillars were swaying so much, that my next thought was that the hotel might collapse, and we had better get the hell out of there. The quake lasted twenty seconds, which seemed like an eternity.

Hotel guests came storming down the stairs from the second and third floors to the lobby. Some went straight to the desk and wanted to check out.

Ten minutes [later], a second shock hit, just as intense as the first. The hotel floor undulated, the pillars swayed, the windows rattled, the low rumble returned, and the entire building squeaked. Ellen and I made a dash for the lobby doors. The quake lasted almost as long as the first.

Many of the Lake Hotel visitors decided not to return to their rooms. Bill Clark, who owned an oil company and usually stayed full summers at the Lake Hotel, bought coffee, tea, donuts and pastries for the hotel guests to be served by Yellowstone Park Company employees. Ellen and I stayed up until 4:30 AM, serving the hotel guests.[12] 99

By 1956, the Lake Hotel had been brought back to life after its near-death experience in the 1940s.

That year, though, the National Park Service (NPS) launched Mission 66, an ambitious decade-long program aimed at bringing national park roads, trails, utilities, campgrounds and structures up to modern-day snuff. By 1966, the fifty-year anniversary of the NPS, more than $1 billion had been spent on park improvements nationwide.

At the project's start, the Yellowstone Park Company (YPC) made recommendations aimed at improving the Lake Hotel, including a heated swimming pool, horseback riding, and a tennis court or golf course.[1] None of this happened, however. Instead, much of the Mission 66 money went toward the construction of Canyon Village at Yellowstone's Grand Canyon.

In fact, after its fairly miraculous resurrection following World War II, the Lake Hotel once again faced an uncertain future. The 1964 Yellowstone Master Plan Study recommended that "at the end of its useful life, the Lake Hotel should be removed and motel-type lodge units substituted."[2]

Things got even shakier in 1966 when the YPC, overwhelmed by the immense financial burden of Mission 66, ended more than six decades of lodging and transportation management by selling out to Goldfield Enterprises. Goldfield then turned around and sold its tourism interests (including the YPC) to General Baking, which morphed into a company called General Host.

General Host, though, virtually ignored the Lake Hotel over the next thirteen years. Structural and safety concerns mostly went without repair. Furniture got dingy. Walls were painted an institutional green.

Alarmingly, a 1969 Master Plan/Design Analysis study of the Lake Hotel recommended an exterior paint job. "The present color scheme of yellow and white is a highly light-reflective one and is in large part responsible for the intrusive effect of this building on the lakeshore,"[3] stated the report. Fortunately, the hotel's distinctive color remained intact.

The hotel limped on, once again faced with an uncertain future.

Opposite: Tourists flocked to Yellowstone in the 1960s, and many stayed at the Lake Hotel—which offered this promotional brochure. *[Photo courtesy of the author]*

Lake Hotel survived the 1960s and 1970s, but concessionaire General Host did little to retain its original charm. This registration desk photograph taken in the 1970s demonstrates the hotel's tacky demise. *[Photo courtesy of the National Park Service, Yellowstone National Park YELL#30219-12a]*

The Hotel Bars

When the hotel finally revved up to speed in the early 1950s, a bar opened in the basement called the Bear Den Saloon. The basement must have been larger then, because these days, it's barely big enough for the hotel's small gift shop storage room, let alone tables and chairs.

Gerald Bateson Jr. writes in his book, *Growing Up in Yellowstone*, that his Uncle Denton and his friends visited the bar annually in the 1950s.

"I always referred to it as the 'dungeon,'" writes Bateson, whose father served as the hotel's winter keeper in the late 1950s and 1960s. "There wasn't a single window for light."[4]

Around 1960, the bar moved upstairs into the hotel's north wing, (today's gift shop location), and the basement next housed the Lake area employee pub—known as The Hole. James Wolfe, author of *A Yellowstone Savage from Fishing Bridge*, who worked three seasons in the 1960s as a

Yellowstone Lake fishing guide, remembers The Hole as being "loud and dark," a place where employees routinely "built beer can pyramids."[5]

These days, it's hard to imagine the light and bright gift shop as a dark and smoky bar. But for

Above: Debby (Anderson) Kearnes, left, and friend, Connie (Semple) Brown, served their fair share of Singapore Slings in 1971, working in the hotel's Rainbow Lounge (today's gift shop). Note the Rainbow Lounge sign (later swiped by Connie) above their heads. *[Photo courtesy of Debby Kearnes]*

Left: This brochure shows some of the services offered to guests in the early 1960s, including a shoe shine stand, dry cleaning and limited room service. *[Photo courtesy of the author]*

BUS TOURS
See transportation agent in lobby.

FISH FRIES
See information desk about Stevenson Island Fish Fry.

FISHING—BOATING
Inquire at main desk. Dock located in front of Hotel.

ICE
Call Hotel operator for bellman desk.

SERVICE STATION
Service station located east of Hotel on main road.

GIFT SHOP
Gift shop located in main lobby.

PICTURE SHOP
Located in lobby.

TELEGRAMS
Telegraph service available at the front desk.

RESERVATIONS
For the park and surrounding area may be made at the front desk.

DRY CLEANING—LAUNDRY
Call Hotel operator for bellman desk.

SHOESHINE
Shoeshine available off lobby.

GENERAL STORE
General store located east of Hotel on Main Road.

SAFE DEPOSIT BOX
We will not be responsible for lost articles. A safe for checking valuables is located at the main desk.

POSTAL SERVICE
Mail drop at front desk; branch post office at Fishing Bridge.

CAR RENTALS
From transportation agent in lobby.

MEDICAL SERVICE
Trained nurses at all areas, hospital west of Hotel.

CHURCH SERVICES
Protestant, Catholic, and Latter-Day-Saints services conducted on Sunday. Please check at information desk for time and place.

PARK INFORMATION
For official information about Yellowstone see ranger at Ranger Station.

MEETINGS—BANQUETS
See the manager for information.

FOOD SERVICE
• Main Dining Room
  Box Lunches
  Available
Hungry?
Call room service for limited menu.

TELEPHONES
Telephones located in the corridors for room service. Long distance from phones in lobby only.

Visit the
Cocktail Lounge
Enjoy the drink of your choice . . . expertly prepared and courteously served. May we suggest the famous

Yellowstone
OLD FASHIONED
or *Yellowstone*
MARTINI

The Cocktail Lounge is located on the main floor, off the dining room.

Other Hotels located at:
• CANYON VILLAGE
• MAMMOTH HOT SPRINGS
• OLD FAITHFUL

Owned and operated by the Yellowstone Park Company.

"I remember a brawl or two, where they had to call the rangers."

two decades or so, it was the place where hotel guests ponied up to a long wooden bar, or sat and chatted at tables, sipping a wide assortment of libations. They also listened to live entertainment, like the Charlie Vedder Jazz Quartet, a group of Ohio State University students who performed regularly there in 1966 and 1967.

For years, the bar was known as the Rainbow Lounge, and it featured western-style swinging doors at the entrance. Debby (Anderson) Kearnes and her dorm roommate, Connie (Semple) Brown, worked here as barmaids in 1971.

"It could get really loud in there," remembers Connie, who now lives in Pullman, Washington. "The hotel didn't put guests in rooms above the bar, because the music really blared at night."[6]

The Rainbow Lounge could also get rowdy.

"I remember a brawl or two, where they had to call the rangers," Connie adds.[7]

Most of the time, though, Debby and Connie just had fun working in the hotel bar—so much so that when the 1971 season ended, Connie decided to take home a keepsake.

"She liberated the Rainbow Lounge sign!" says Debby, who met her husband, Jim Kearnes, in the lounge, and married him in 1973.[8]

Yep, admits Connie, she stole the sign—mostly because the bar's name was being changed to the Dry Dock Lounge. "The sign hangs in my kitchen, except when I bring it back to the hotel for reunions," she says.[9]

After the bar was renamed the Dry Dock, it served as the hotel watering hole until the 1980s; the bar has since been relocated to the left of the dining room entrance. And the gift shop, which before existed in a glass-walled room wedged between today's registration desk and the lobby grandfather clock, finally settled into its current home next to the fireplace.

Hotel Held Magic for Many Employees

In summer of 1969, as the Vietnam War raged on, and the Lake Hotel struggled to survive, Debby Anderson—then called "Whitey"—worked as a waitress in the hotel's dining room.

She wore, in her words, an "ugly" uniform, which consisted of either a lime-green, Pepto-Bismol pink, or "putrid" gold skirt, a white blouse, a white Dutch-girl apron, and a name tag shaped like a bus.

Debby worked six days a week, for $1.10 an hour; $3.50 a day for room and board was deducted from her salary. But she liked the job,

Yellowstone Company Names

The name of the company that has managed Yellowstone's hotels has changed many times since 1883—which can be a little confusing. To help sort things out, here's a list that chronicles the companies that have managed the Lake Hotel and other park hotels:

- **1883–1886:** Yellowstone Park Improvement Company (YPIC). The park's first attempt at lodging went bankrupt.

- **1886–1909:** Yellowstone Park Association (YPA). By 1907, Harry Child owned the YPA, which his family ran until 1966.

- **1909–1936:** Yellowstone Park Hotel Company (YPHCo). Harry Child formed this offshoot of the YPA to strictly manage the park's hotels. Park lodges were managed separately.

- **1936–1979:** Yellowstone Park Company (YPC). The Harry Child-William Nichols family continued to manage the park's lodging until 1966, when they sold out to Goldfield Enterprises, which soon became part of General Host, Inc. The company kept the YPC name.

- **1979–1995:** TW Recreational Services. In 1979 the United States government purchased Yellowstone lodging, and awarded the concessionaire contract to Trans World Airlines (TWA) Services, Inc.—which later became Trans World (TW) Services and finally Trans World (TW) Recreational Services.

- **1995–2002:** Amfac Parks & Resorts. Amfac acquired TW Recreational Services in 1995.

- **2002–present:** Xanterra Parks & Resorts. Amfac is renamed Xanterra in 2002.

[Photo courtesy of the author]

> **"We would sing two or three songs and then rush back to the kitchen to pick up our orders."**

Above Left: "Guests dined at wooden tables that had little placemats, each decorated with a caricature map of the park," says Debby (Anderson) Kearnes, shown here second from the right. "Evenings, the tables had paper tablecloths in [the] autumn colors of gold and green."[15] *[Photo courtesy of Debby Kearnes]*

Above Right: Nightly, in the late 1960s, the hotel's waitstaff would stop serving every thirty minutes to gather around the piano and organ to perform for diners. *[Photo courtesy of Debby Kearnes]*

so much that she returned in 1970 to wait tables and in 1971 to serve drinks in the hotel's western-themed Rainbow Lounge.

"The hotel had a reputation of faded glory—second fiddle to the Old Faithful and Mammoth hotels," says Debby, who now lives in Seattle with her husband, Jim Kearnes. He worked as a Yellowstone Lake fishing guide from 1966 to 1969.

"But we loved it here."[10]

In those days, Debby says the yellow dining room was decorated with heavy floral drapes that dated back to the 1940s or so. Paper tablecloths covered the wood tables, and the simple menu featured everything from fried chicken for $2.95 to New York steak for $5.25.[11]

Debby says the sunroom did not have its signature grand piano, but the dining room had both an upright piano and an organ—around which the waitstaff gathered every thirty minutes or so to perform.

"We would sing two or three songs and then

rush back to the kitchen to pick up our orders, and listen to the cooks yell at us for being late," she remembers.[12]

Debby lived her first two seasons in the Sandpiper dorm with Connie (Semple) Brown and Caroline Poplaski. Debby recalls that a dorm matron named Macy tried to keep boys out, "but she was about one hundred and ten and deaf as a post. She would just yell up the stairs and curse at us for being noisy and slovenly."[13]

Debby and her Yellowstone friends have held several reunions, and she and her husband visit the park frequently.

"The hotel's still the same," Debby says wistfully. "It's nicer now, but it's the same. Every morning when I worked here, I would walk up and down the long carpet in the lobby, and look out the windows. I could see Mount Sheridan and the whole Absaroka mountain range.

"This was my view," she adds. "It's still my view."[14]

During the 1960s and 1970s, the hotel's glass-walled gift shop was located in the lobby near the registration desk. Items sold in 1968 included handcrafted Indian arts; moccasins and fancy linens.
[Photo courtesy of the National Park Service, Yellowstone National Park YELL#30219-13a]

The National Government Saves the Lake Hotel

In 1979, disgusted by General Host's lackluster management of the Yellowstone Park Company (YPC), the national government finally stepped in and took control of Yellowstone's concessions, including lodging and transportation. By that point, the park's hotels were, according to the National Park Service, "even barely adequate, much less quality concession facilities."

In 1978, park service inspectors had found deficiencies in the Lake Hotel's plumbing, elevators, roof, foundations, and electrical system. The hotel's fire exits, alarm systems, and fire sprinkler system also needed repairs. Most alarming, consultants discovered a fault in the foundation that could have caused the hotel to collapse. They deemed the structure unsafe for occupancy, adding that continued use could "result in tragedy."

The government paid General Host $19.9 million for the YPC and awarded Trans World Airlines (TWA) Services a two-year interim contract to run park concession operations. In 1981, TWA Services (renamed TW Services) received a ten-year contract that required 22 percent of the company's gross revenue— in addition to all pretax profits over 5 percent— be spent on park capital improvements.

After fifty years of second-class status, the Lake Hotel again received respect, and a shot at its original elegance.

Above: Most of the hotel guest rooms were fairly simple in the 1970s. This lake-facing room, for instance, features a sink—which means guests used a communal bathroom down the hall. Also notice the wood floors; today's rooms have carpeting. *(Photo courtesy of the National Park Service, Yellowstone National Park YELL#30223-09]*

Left: The wicker furniture that long defined the hotel's sunroom is mostly missing in this circa 1970 photograph. Instead, large less-than-attractive couches—previously used in the Canyon Hotel—dominate the lounge. *[Photo courtesy of the National Park Service, Yellowstone National Park YELL#30223-16]*

Hotel Restores its 1891 Soul

A funny thing happened after TWA Services came on board in 1979: The traveling public, which had shunned big, fancy hotels for decades, suddenly liked them again.

This worked out rather well for the Lake Hotel, which had survived fifty years of lackluster patronage and at least three advocated demolitions. Suddenly the hotel that had stood longest in an American national park was popular again.

A multi-million dollar restoration launched in 1981 took a decade to complete. Beyond major structural repairs, the hotel received fresh indoor paint—azalea, mint and shell rose colors—and furniture, like brass beds, meant to evoke 1890s charm. Best of all, the sunroom's wicker furniture, which had been scattered throughout the park "in warehouses...kids' dormitories...all over the place"[18] was rounded up and renovated.

Other changes: the gift shop moved from the lobby to its current location, and the bar was relocated to the left of the dining room entrance, where it remains today. The dining room, which had operated more or less as a coffee shop, regained its former upscale identity, and now featured refurbished chairs, fanned cloth napkins, and stemmed crystal. Chefs prepared more sophisticated entrees, like fresh seafood, and "such things as flaming desserts...[fare] that people expect at a fine hotel."[16]

The lodging also got a fresh name: The Lake Yellowstone Hotel. Better yet, it earned a spot on the National Register of Historic Places—protecting its survival for years to come.

On May 21, 1991, a "Culinary Tribute to a Grand Hotel" was held to celebrate the hotel's renovation, and its 100th anniversary. Guests dined on "Roast Tenderloin of Beef with Wild Mushrooms Duxelle" and "Dauphine Potatoes," and enjoyed the after-dinner entertainment provided by Native American troubadour Jack Gladstone, and big band musicians, Shelly and the Allen Brothers.

The Grand Lady waltzed in celebration.

Left: The Lake Hotel sunroom again featured wicker furniture in the 1980s after a major renovation. *[Photo courtesy of Xanterra Parks & Resorts]*

Above Left: Lake Yellowstone Hotel sign *[Photo courtesy of Joshua D. Stein]*

The minute the hotel closed for the season in September 2012, workmen began ripping the wood floor out of the hotel's sunroom. Swiftly, decisively, a two-year, $28.5 million renovation began.

The first phase included a complete overhaul of the lobby, sunroom, and dining room. The registration and bell desks also got makeovers, and a concierge desk emerged, tucked in next to the Colonial-style staircase. A dark wood, sit-down bar sprang up beside the dining room entrance.

Upstairs in the hotel's original Old House, the hallways and forty-three rooms got new everything, including colors, furnishings, and lighting. Four suites went in, and the Presidential Suite, which debuted in 1924, was transformed from a dated enclave into a luxury hideaway.

The renovation's second phase started at the close of the summer 2013 season, and included the stripping and redesigning of one hundred and thirty-four rooms and corridors in the hotel's east wing. The deli received a fresh look and menu, as well as an expanded seating area.

A&E Architects of Missoula, Montana, oversaw the historical renovation, which emphasized the preservation of original material. All of the hotel's original windows, for instance, most with traditional rope-and-pulley systems, were painstakingly removed and repaired.

Finally, in July, 2014, to the delight of guests, Yellowstone's most extravagant hotel was fully unveiled. It was a déjà vu moment, gloriously mimicking the hotel's 1929 completion.

Opposite: A legion of workers toiled through two winters, 2012-13 and 2013-14, enduring sub-degree temperatures, to totally refurbish the hotel. *[Photo courtesy of Kat Brekken]*

Above: The entire hotel was gutted down to the studs. "We put in new concrete footings, new columns, and in some areas, new structural beams,"[1] says John Simpson, a carpenter foreman with the renovation project's general contractor, Dick Anderson Construction of Bozeman, Montana. *[Photo courtesy of the author]*

[Photos courtesy of Joshua D. Stein]

A Brand-New Bar

The bar has moved several times in the hotel's history. In 1895, a connecting two-room bar, located in front of today's gift shop, required guests sit in one room and for servers to obtain liquor from the other. After World War II, guests sipped their libations inside the room that now houses the gift shop; the bar was originally called the Rainbow Lounge and then the Dry Dock Lounge. In the 1980s, a small bar appeared next to the dining room entrance; it's now been replaced by a horseshoe-shaped bar surrounded by barstool seating.

A Beautiful Dining Room

Chefs pamper guests in the hotel's 250-seat dining room, often touted as the park's finest, preparing such delicacies as "Montana Natural Lamb," "Prosciutto-Wrapped Pork Tenderloin," and the vegetarian pasta dish, "Orecchiette." Lake-facing windows line the restaurant, but the table to request—118—offers the most expansive bay window views of Yellowstone Lake and the Absaroka Mountain Range.

Center Lobby Spruced Up

Architect Robert Reamer originally intended the hotel's center lobby to be more of a gem: a glass-encased atrium connecting the 1903–04 middle section with the 1923 east wing. That didn't happen, but the recent renovation definitely dolled up this lobby, which now offers improved passenger and service elevators, as well as two old-fashioned phone booths—popular because of sketchy cell phone service in the lake area.

The expansive Presidential Suite, with its 180-degree view of the lake and forest, may be the hotel's best deal for large parties, providing two full bedrooms (with separate hallway entrances); two full bathrooms (master bath has a two-person soaking tub with a lake view!), and a living room, complete with a hideaway sofa bed—for less than the price of two standard hotel rooms. *[Photo courtesy of the author]*

Famous Guests

The Lake Hotel, of course, has had its share of well-known guests. Among them:

The First Lady lunched with friends in the hotel dining room. *[Photo courtesy of the George W. Bush Presidential Library and Museum]*

- Actor Beau Bridges, 1979
- Newsman Tom Brokaw, 2001
- First Lady Laura Bush, 2002
- Comedian Buddy Hackett, 1988
- Actor Steve Martin, 1982
- Actress Ann Miller, 1990s
- Singer Donnie Osmond, 1988
- Western stars Roy Rogers and Dale Evans, 1963
- Actress Marion Ross, 1985
- Chicken king Colonel Sanders, 1978
- Media mogul Ted Turner, 2014

Heeeere's Dale! Lake Hotel's Winter Keeper

Dale Fowler doesn't look a thing like Jack Nicholson, but some folks want to make that chilling connection.

Fowler—long, lean, quiet—has been the winter keeper at the Lake Hotel every year but two since 1987. He shovels giant snow blocks off roofs, patrols hotel corridors for critter invaders, and basically guards against unanticipated disaster.

No, Fowler says, he's nothing like demented author Jack Torrance in the horror classic *The Shining*, who hacked into the hotel bathroom—where his wife cowered—and maniacally announced, "Heeeere's Johnny!"

He scoffs at the comparison.

"That movie wasn't realistic at all," says Fowler. "You can't run the heat in a big hotel in winter. It makes the snow melt off the roof and create a giant ice sheet over the side. Nothing would wear a hotel down faster."[2]

Fowler, an Arkansas native—who maybe saw an inch of snow each winter growing up—has zero Hollywood ambitions. He's a self-admitted loner who savors the calm, quiet, and aloneness of Yellowstone winters. He sees an occasional animal, but mostly it's just him making the daily rounds, ensuring all lake-area buildings are safe and sound.

"People think I have an exciting, romantic job, but it's actually pretty routine,"[3] says Fowler, whose life picks up in summer, when he manages the hotel's maintenance department.

> **"**One night a security guard said he saw a Victorian woman floating down the hallway in the east wing.**"**

Winter keeper Dale Fowler says he has to pace himself, working in temperatures that can dip as low as forty degrees below zero. "I always tell my bosses [that] I don't work according to a calendar or a clock," he says. "I work as needed, and depending on weather conditions."[8] After scaling a hotel roof, Fowler uses a long saw to slice through blocks of snow, and a shovel to push them off. "It requires muscle," he admits with a shrug.[9] *[Photo courtesy of Crystal Cassidy]*

The winters of 2012–13 and 2013–14 totally rattled his routine. Upwards of one hundred workmen were on site daily, renovating the hotel. "My house was at ground zero," says Fowler, who lives a snowball-throw away from the hotel. "Men were working here from 6:30 in the morning to 8:30 at night. It definitely disrupted my peace and quiet."[4]

He does allow, however, that the renovation greatly improved the hotel.

Once a month in winter, Fowler hops on a snowmobile and varooms two hours away to West Yellowstone to buy perishables. He also visits Old Faithful Snow Lodge, where his longtime girlfriend, Crystal Cassidy, runs the winter ski shop. For fun, he watches football on his satellite television (he's a rabid University of Arkansas Razorbacks fan), or he straps on skis

and slides out on the frozen lake.

"The lake sings," he says. "The ice has cracks in it, and warm air causes the big cracks to move. When you're skiing across the lake, that noise is scary as hell."[5]

Speaking of scary, Fowler's likely heard more ghost stories, from guests and employees, than anyone else. Like the multiple times a guest's bathtub supposedly filled with water—when nobody was in the room. And the time a night porter heard footsteps repeatedly creak across a hotel storage room—again, when nobody was in the room. Or the time that a cop from New Jersey said he heard voices coming out of the wall in his room.

"One night a security guy said he saw a Victorian woman floating down the hallway in the east wing," Fowler says. "If you believe

in ghosts, you're going to see one."[6]

Fowler says he sometimes thinks about retiring—but not yet. He admits the hotel and Yellowstone Lake both have an emotional hold on him.

"There's a certain pride in working here," he says. "You take it personally, keeping the buildings as nice as you can."

"I like to think of it as my hotel."[7]

Catherine Foley Grandly Entertains

The camper truck rolls under the porte cochère, and Catherine Foley—in a dark short-sleeved blouse and black ankle-brushing skirt—hops out and scurries into the Lake Hotel.

Her soft-spoken husband, Patrick, soon follows, depositing armfuls of sheet music next to a piano bench in the hotel's well-lit sunroom. Carefully, he peels the protective vinyl cover from the 1923 Knabe grand piano, and his wife takes a seat at the keyboard.

When the lobby's grandfather clock strikes six o'clock, Foley's fingers strike ivory—and the Lake Hotel's evening officially begins.

"I try to play crowd pleasers," says Foley, who guesses that she plays one hundred and fifty songs a night, most from memory. "Songs from *Phantom of the Opera*, *Les Misérables*—all the show tunes. The guests love the show tunes. But I also play the classic standards, like 'Over the Rainbow' and 'Moonlight Sonata.'

"I get a lot of requests," she adds. "I try to play anything that a guest would like to hear."[10]

It's a musical ritual that has blessed evenings here since 2003. Foley, a retired math teacher, applied for the job after vacationing summers in Yellowstone with her family; she and Patrick have visited the park nearly every year they have been married.

Foley typically entertains five nights a week, except mid-June to mid-August, when the

Above: Pianist Catherine Foley says that only once has the show almost not gone on: "One year, eight men were moving the piano, and they dropped it, and the pedals broke off. It was the day before the season opened. Fortunately, our wood shop was able to make new wooden supports [for the pedals] and paint them black to match the piano—in time for opening."[12] *[Photo courtesy of the author]*

Left: At dusk, bellmen typically lower the hotel flag while pianist Catherine Foley plays patriotic songs. In May 2014, however, Miss Idaho, Sarah Downs (right), and Miss Montana, Sheridan Pope, handled the ritual. *[Photo courtesy of the author]*

The Lake String Quartet includes (from left) Colleen Tan, violin; Timothy Tan, violin; Martha Colby, cello; and Leanne Darling, viola. The group plays four hours, five nights a week, at the far end of the historic sunroom—in front of the windows—offering guests a lake view during their performance. *[Photo courtesy of the author]*

Lake String Quartet graces the hotel. Then the blonde-haired mother of five grown children performs two evenings and three afternoons.

When Foley's not playing, she and Patrick often fly-fish, either on the park's Firehole River or south in the Grand Tetons.

Foley says she hopes to keep on entertaining until 2023.

"We just love Yellowstone, and playing at the hotel is such a pleasure," she says. "It's really like home. Why would I ever want to leave?"[11]

Sweet Strings of Summer

At the height of Yellowstone's summer season, as the sun etches its farewell, the sound of stringed instruments wafts through the Lake Hotel.

Indeed, the hotel has a resident string quartet, and a marvelous one at that. No one can remember how far back the tradition of a summer-playing string quartet stretches—but the guess is decades. Current violinist Timothy Tan came on board in 1996, and says that the group received its current name, the Lake String

Quartet, the following year.

The quartet plays from mid-June to mid-August, dazzling guests with a diverse repertoire designed to please all ears: a little bit of classical, a dollop of pop, perhaps the hand-clapping "Hoe-Down" from Aaron Copland's *Rodeo*.

"Every night is like a concert,"[13] says the tall, slender Tan, who—like the rest of the quartet—plays professionally when not at the Lake Hotel.

"We are always trying to engage the room,"[14] says petite violinist Colleen Tan, who started dating Tim in 2000; they married in 2001, after Tim proposed on the beach in front of the Lake Hotel. Their two young children spend summers with them in Yellowstone.

"If we play Beethoven and [the people in the audience] like it, we play more classics," she says. "But we never stay on one genre too long."[15]

As much as they switch up their nightly performances, the quartet always ends on the same note. It is their trademark song—an upbeat tune that sends guests to their rooms, humming:

"Happy Trails."

The Return of the Historic Yellow Bus

By the early 1970s, Yellowstone had sold all but one of its Model 706 Yellow Buses, believing them to be passé. But in 2001, when Alaska's Skagway Street Car Company offered Yellowstone the chance to buy back eight historic buses, park leaders jumped (and then paid nearly $40,000 for each bus).

TransGlobal Design & Manufacturing in Livonia, Michigan, handled renovations, modernizing everything under the hood, including the addition of a 5.4-liter Ford engine. An automatic transmission replaced the old double clutch, and power steering was added. The roll-back roof's now made of a vinyl-material instead of canvas, and aluminum upgraded the wood floor. An added speaker system helps passengers better hear the tour guide/driver.

Buses returned to service in 2007, shuttling guests on mostly shorter, specialty tours.

Above: Lisa Culpepper, who guides both the Photo Safari and Lake Butte Sunset tours, returns from a morning tour in Mason City, one of Yellowstone's eight Historic Yellow Buses. *[Photo courtesy of the author]*

Right: Photo Safari guide Doug Hilborn helps guest Moses Solorzano with a lens filter during the morning tour. *[Photo courtesy of the author]*

Summers at the Lake Hotel, a Historic Yellow Bus sits beneath the porte cochère, unless it's out and about for the morning Photo Safari Tour or the evening Lake Butte Sunset Tour.

The price tag to renovate each Historic Yellow Bus: a cool $250,000.[16]

Christmas in Yellowstone

Every summer, on August 25, the Lake Hotel—like the rest of the park—celebrates Christmas in Yellowstone.

It's tough to pinpoint exactly how this celebration started. One story says that a summer blizzard stranded guests at the Old Faithful Inn in the early 1900s, and the winter weather inspired an impromptu Christmas celebration—but weather records prove otherwise.[17] More likely, the annual event sprouted in the 1950s from another employee summer shindig known as Savage Days.

However it started, guests and employees love Christmas in Yellowstone. Gift shops deck the halls with decorations, the employee dining rooms serve traditional Yuletide fare, and impromptu Christmas trees pop up all over the park.

As Yellowstone employees have recited for decades: "Christmas Comes But Twice a Year—Once at Home and Once Up Here."

Lake Hotel gift-shop employees celebrate Christmas in Yellowstone, 2014. *[Photo courtesy of the author]*

> Gift shops deck the halls with decorations, the employee dining rooms serve traditional Yuletide fare, and impromptu Christmas trees pop up all over the park.

Snow often blankets the grounds surrounding the Lake Hotel when it opens for the summer season each year in mid-May. *[Photo courtesy of the author]*

A National Historical Landmark

In 1991, in commemoration of a miraculous recovery and a happy 100th birthday, the Lake Hotel earned herself a spot in the National Register of Historic Places.

Twenty-five years later, as the Grand Lady of the Lake celebrates her 125th anniversary, the hotel has now been named a National Historic Landmark, a designation of much distinction. Of the more than 85,000 places in the United States that have been named as Historic Places, only about 2,500 have been elevated to the status of Historic Landmark.

A celebration commemorating the hotel's renovation and landmark status was held in June, 2014. Jim McCaleb, vice president and general manager of Xanterra Parks and Resorts—Yellowstone's primary concessionaire in charge of lodging and transportation—and Yellowstone National Park Superintendent Dan Wenk both spoke at the event, held in front of the hotel.

"This is a great day in Yellowstone," Wenk said. "What better way to honor the anniversary than to designate the hotel as a National Historic Landmark, and usher in the next 125 years of grandeur for the Lake Hotel."[18]

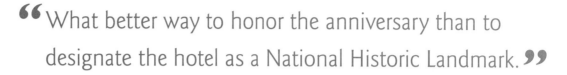

"What better way to honor the anniversary than to designate the hotel as a National Historic Landmark."

Xanterra Vice President and General Manager Jim McCaleb, center, and Yellowstone National Park Superintendent Dan Wenk cut the symbolic ribbon commemorating the hotel's most recent renovation. Bellman Andrew Sonoras looks on. *[Photo courtesy of the author]*

In celebration of everything that the Lake Hotel has been... let's all raise a glass and toast Yellowstone's hotel with a view.

Above: Architect Robert Reamer wanted guests to fully enjoy the views offered by the Lake Hotel. He no doubt envisioned the relaxing "Ahhhhhs" his 180-degree-view lounge would inspire, then...and now. *[Photo courtesy of the author]*

Opposite: Guests in early days were assigned a departure time for their bus and—luggage in hand—typically assembled under the porte cochère, in excited anticipation of more adventures in Wonderland. *[Photo courtesy of the National Park Service, Yellowstone National Park YELL#25004]*

Always, Forever:
The Grand Lady of the Lake

Now, as the hotel prepares for its 125th anniversary in 2016, the time has come to celebrate such a spectacular achievement.

By all accounts, the Lake Hotel should be gone, dead—a burning rubble of historical firewood. More than once, park leaders deemed the rambling yellow structure obsolete, past its prime, a candidate for demolition.

Fate kept her alive.

Today Yellowstone Lake—constant and full of life—continues to charm. The Absaroka Mountain Range undulates across the horizon. Lodgepole pines quiver in the afternoon winds.

Bears, once nightly guests at the hotel's dump, rarely visit now. But bison, elk, and deer regularly skirt the hotel, attracting visitors' eyes and wonder—much like the bears did in the early 1900s.

And so, in celebration of everything that the Lake Hotel has been and everything that it will be, let's all raise a glass and toast Yellowstone's hotel with a view.

The Grand Lady of the Lake.

REFERENCES

Note: The sources used throughout this book are varied, including miscellaneous materials gathered from the Yellowstone Heritage and Research Center and other related collections. Many details are a matter of common historic record, while other facts were gleaned from available resources to the best of the author's knowledge and research. If you have anything else to add or find any discrepancies, please get in touch with the author at www.michelletrappen.com.

Chapter 1: A Hotel Rises

1. Superintendent's Annual Report for Yellowstone National Park, 1887, Yellowstone Heritage and Research Center (YHRC) Library.
2. "The Inflation Calculator (1800-2014)," Consumer Price Index: *Historical Statistics of the United States* (USGPO, 1975), www.westegg.com
3. Carrie Adell Strahorn, *Fifteen Thousand Miles By Stage*, New York/London: G. P. Putnam's Sons/Knickerbocker Press, 1911, PDF e-book.
4. Letter from F. A. Boutelle to John W. Noble, Secretary of the Interior (May 9, 1890), bound volume: "Letters Sent Aug. 18, 1889 to June 25, 1892," YHRC Archives, 91-92.
5. Barbara H. Dittl and Joanne Mallmann, "Plain to Fancy: The Lake Hotel, 1889-1929," *Montana: The Magazine of Western History*, spring 1984, 35.
6. Ibid
7. Ibid
8. Ibid, 36
9. Ibid, The Inflation Calculator

Chapter 2: The Grand Tour

1. Aubrey Haines, *The Yellowstone Story: A History of Our First National Park, Volume Two* (revised edition), (Colorado: University Press of Colorado, 1996), 104.

2. Clarence D. Long, *Wages and Earnings in the United States, 1860-1890: Wages by Occupational and Individual Characteristics*, (Princeton University Press, 1960), www.nber.org/chapters/c2500
3. Sign up for a Yellowstone Tally-Ho stagecoach ride at any park activity desk, or call Yellowstone National Park Lodges reservations at 1-866-439-7375.
4. "The Yellowstone Park Hotel," *Bozeman Avant-Courier*, April 5, 1883, 1. Found on microfilm, YHRC Library.
5. Ibid, Haines, 107-08
6. 1908 stagecoach robbery file, YPC records, YHRC Archives.
7. Ibid
8. Ibid
9. Ibid
10. I found this poem in the YHRC Archives (1908 stagecoach robbery file) but was unable to track down any more information on it or Miss Halle. If you have additional information, please contact me at michelletrappen.com.
11. Ibid, The Inflation Calculator
12. Mark Miller, "Cruising Yellowstone Lake 'The Wylie Way' in 1903," www.yellowstonegate.com/tag/hester-henshall
13. Ibid, Haines, 126
14. Adrian Jawort, "Genocide by Other Means: U.S. Army Slaughtered Buffalo in Plains Indian Wars," *Indian Country*, May 9, 2011, http://indiancountrytodaymedianetwork.com/2011/05/09/genocide-other-means-us-army-slaughtered-buffalo-plains-indian-wars-30798
15. www.texas-best.com/tag/lonesomedove
16. "Chronicling America: Historic American Newspapers, Library of Congress," *The Helena Independent* April 27, 1891, http://chroniclingamerica.loc.gov/
17. Superintendent's Annual Report for Yellowstone National Park, 1892, YHRC Library.
18. Richard Bartlett, *Yellowstone: A Wilderness Besieged*, (University of Arizona Press, 1989), 193.

19. Schedule of prices of the Yellowstone Park Association, "cigars, tobacco, etc.," YPC records, YHRC Archives.

20. James Mote and A. Berle Clemensen, "Historic structures report: Lake Hotel, Lake Lodge, Roosevelt Lodge, Old Faithful Lodge, Yellowstone National Park, Wyoming," YHRC Library.

21. Mark Miller, "Through Yellowstone by Coach—1904," a story by Stephen M. Dale, *Adventures In Yellowstone: Early Travelers Tell Their Tales*, (Guilford, Connecticut: The Globe Pequot Press, 2009), 254.

22. "Lake Kitchen," YPC records, Series II: Correspondence, Sub-series: Business, YHRC Archives.

23. Ben Pierce, "Uncle Tom's Trail: Hike into Grand Canyon of the Yellowstone a Trip Through History," *Bozeman Daily Chronicle*, July 31, 2011.

24. Superintendent's Annual Report for Yellowstone National Park, 1890, YHRC Library.

Chapter 3: The Lake "Colonial" Hotel

1. Ruth Quinn, *Weaver of Dreams: The Life and Architecture of Robert C. Reamer,* (Bozeman: Leslie and Ruth Quinn, 2004), 19.

2. Ibid, 20

3. Ibid, 25

4. Ibid, 50

5. Ibid, The Inflation Calculator

6. Reau Campbell, *Complete Guide and Descriptive Book of the Yellowstone Park*, (Chicago: H.E. Klamer, 1913), 158

Chapter 4: Enter the Automobile

1. Ibid, Bartlett, 84

2. Ibid

3. "Governing the Admission of Automobiles for the Season of 1915," Superintendent's Annual Report for Yellowstone National Park, 1915, YHRC Archives.

4. Ibid

5. Letter to potential guests from Huntley Child of the Yellowstone Park Hotel Company, June 5, 1916, YPC records, YHRC Archives.

6. Yellowstone Park Boat Company, proposed schedule of rates, approved April 15, 1912, YPC records, YHRC Archives.

7. *The National Parks: America's Best Idea* can be viewed on Netflix (under documentaries) or by going to www.pbs.org/nationalparks/.

Chapter 5: The Finishing Touches

1. "The U.S. Inflation Calculator," 1913-2015, www.usinflationcalculator.com

2. Information provided by the Lake Yellowstone Hotel paint crew, 2014.

3. R. Laurie Simmons and Thomas H. Simmons, "Lake Hotel," *National Historic Landmark Nomination*, March 2014, 5.

4. Ibid, Dittl and Mallmann, 4

5. Letter from Yellowstone Park Superintendent Horace Albright to Park President William Nichols, Aug. 12, 1926, YPC records, YHRC Archives.

6. Ibid, Haines, 107

7. Ruth Quinn, author of *Weaver of Dreams: The Life and Architecture of Robert C. Reamer*, worked at the Lake Hotel in 1993 when the Carters visited. "They did stay at least two nights in Lake Hotel," she says in a personal communication. "They ate in the dining room the first night. The second [night] the pub was opened early for their private dinner. They declined the company's offer to use the Presidential suite, which would have required the guests who had reserved to move elsewhere. The Carters elected to stay in a regular lakeside room instead of inconveniencing others."

8. Letter from Stephen Mather, director of the National Park Service, to Horace Albright, Yellowstone park superintendent, Sept. 20, 1924, YPC records, YHRC Archives.

9. Ibid, The U.S. Inflation Calculator

10. Ibid

11. Ibid

12. Ibid

Chapter 6: The Dark Years

1. Letter from Wyoming rancher Irving Larom to Park President William Nichols, Dec. 12, 1931, YPC records, YHRC Archives.

2. Ibid, The U.S. Inflation Calculator

3. Letter from Park President William Nichols to Guy Edwards, acting superintendent of Yellowstone National Park, June 4, 1932, YPC records, YHRC Archives.

4. Letter from Park President William Nichols to Judge John H. Edwards, U.S. Department of the Interior, July 6, 1932, YPC records, YHRC Archives.

5. Letter from architect Robert Reamer to Park President William Nichols, Oct. 18, 1934, YPC records, YHRC Archives.

6. Periodical reports on hotels, 1937 and 1938, Yellowstone Park Company, YPC records, YHRC Archives.

7. Ibid, The U.S. Inflation Calculator

8. Letter from architect Robert Reamer to Park President William Nichols, Aug. 3, 1935, YPC records, YHRC Archives.

9. Ibid, The U.S. Inflation Calculator

10. Letter from architect Robert Reamer to Park President William Nichols, Aug. 3, 1935, YPC records, YHRC Archives.

11. Letter from J. Higgins of Stroheim & Romann to Floyd Mueller of the Yellowstone Park Company, June 13, 1939, YPC records, YHRC Archives.

12. Letter from Park President William Nichols to vendor Hazel Wray Davey, July 3, 1939, YPC records, YHRC Archives.

13. Letter from attorney Vilroy C. Miller of Livingston, Montana, to Park President William Nichols, March 4, 1941, YPC records, YHRC Archives.

14. Letter from Park President William Nichols to Howard Hays of the Glacier Park Transportation Company, July 13, 1951, YPC records, YHRC Archives.

15. Letter from Yellowstone attorney Hugh D. Galusha to J. P. Marstella, Internal Revenue Service agent, Jan. 18, 1940, YPC records, YHRC Archives.

16. Ibid, Haynes, 479

17. Memorandum for the Superintendent, Yellowstone National Park, issued by the United States Department of the Interior, Aug. 13, 1943, regarding visit by Rear Admiral L. Sheldon, Jr., YPC Records, YHRC Archives.

18. www.nationalparktraveler.com/2010/11/navy-converted-yosemites-luxurious-ahwahnee-hotel-hospital-use-during-world-war-ii7269

Chapter 7: Staying Alive

1. "A Special Announcement from Yellowstone National Park," Aug. 30, 1945, YPC records, YHRC Archives.

2. Ibid, Haines, 479

3. Letter from Park President William Nichols to Yellowstone attorney Hugh D. Galusha, Nov. 26, 1952, YPC records, YHRC Archives.

4. "Expenditures to Improve Lake Hotel," 1947-1953, Lake Hotel 1952-1958 file, YPC records, YHRC Archives.

5. "Details of Additions to Buildings & Equipment, 1950 Season," Yellowstone Park Company, Hotel Division-Equipment, Lake Hotel, YPC Records, YHRC Archives.

6. Ibid, "Operating Income—Hotel Division, 1950 Season."

7. Ibid, The U.S. Inflation Calculator

8. Schedule of rates brochure, 1953, Yellowstone Park Company, YPC records, YHRC Archives.

9. Letter from architect Robert Reamer to Park President William Nichols, Oct. 18, 1934, YPC records, YHRC Archives.

10. Ibid, letter from William Nichols to Howard Hays

11. Email to author from Lloyd Wood (former Lake Lodge cook), Feb. 10, 2015.

12. Dick Crysdale, *Yellowstone, Cutthroats and Me: A Fishing Guide's Autobiography*, (WordsWorth, 2009), 65-66.

Chapter 8: Going the Distance

1. "Study of Yellowstone Park Company's Concessions in Yellowstone National Park," May 26, 1958, YPC records, YHRC Archives.

2. "Yellowstone Master Plan Study prepared by the Yellowstone Study Committee," 1964, YPC records, YHRC Library.

3. "Master Plan for the Preservation and Use of Yellowstone National Park, Wyoming," Volume I, Chapter 5, Design Analysis, Lake Hotel Development, prepared by T. J. Wirth, YPC records, YHRC Library.

4. Gerald L. Bateson Jr., *Growing Up in Yellowstone*, (2011: Pumice Point Press, Gardiner, Montana), 72

5. Email to author from James O. Wolfe (former Yellowstone boat guide), May 6, 2015.

6. Author interview with Connie Semple Brown (former Lake Hotel barmaid), July 4, 2015.

7. Ibid

8. Author interview with Debby Anderson Kearnes (former Lake Hotel waitress/barmaid), July 21, 2014.

9. Ibid, Brown interview

10. Ibid, Kearnes interview

11. A Lake Hotel menu, 1960s, provided by Connie Semple Brown.

12. Ibid, Kearnes interview

13. Ibid

14. Ibid

15. Ibid

16. Buzzy Hassrick, "Historic Lake Hotel Restored," *Casper Star-Tribune*, May 24, 1984, YPC records, YHRC Archives.

Chapter 9: Full Circle

1. Author interview with John Simpson (carpenter foreman), June 14, 2014.

2. Author interview with Dale Fowler (winter keeper), Sept., 27, 2014.

3. Ibid

4. Ibid

5. Ibid

6. Ibid

7. Ibid

8. Ibid

9. Ibid

10. Author interview with Catherine Foley (pianist), July 12, 2014.

11. Ibid

12. Ibid

13. Author interview with Timothy Tan (violinist), Aug. 9, 2014.

14. Author interview with Colleen Tan (violinist), Aug. 9, 2014.

15. Ibid

16. Robert Goss, "Geyser Bob's Yellowstone Park History Service," http://geyserbob.org/Buses-White.html

17. Leslie Quinn, "Savage Christmas...the Best of Times," *Yellowstone Science: A Quarterly Publication Devoted to the Natural and Cultural Resources*, Volume 9, Issue 3, 2001.

18. Yellowstone Park Superintendent Dan Wenk, speaking at the Lake Yellowstone Hotel dedication, June 23, 2014.

ABOUT THE AUTHOR

Michelle Trappen grew up in Redondo Beach, California. She studied journalism at Redondo Union High School, and then at California State University, Fullerton. Feature writing jobs followed at the *Orange County Register, Fort Worth Star-Telegram* and *The Oregonian* in Portland, Oregon. She spent twenty one years at *The Oregonian*, writing about people, places, and interests, and specializing in small town journalism.

Michelle left *The Oregonian* in 2008, and in 2012—on a whim—came to Yellowstone. Fate placed her at the Lake Hotel, where she's worked as a concierge, hotel tour guide and historic yellow bus driver and guide. Her work showed her the need for a book about the oldest hotel originally built in America's national park system.

And thus, *Grand Lady of the Lake* was born.